with photographs by the *Evening Gazette*, Blackpool

Carnegie Publishing, 1992

Railways of the Fylde

by Barry McLoughlin

First edition, 1992

Copyright © Barry McLoughlin, 1992

Published by Carnegie Publishing Ltd., 18 Maynard St., Preston
Designed and typeset in Baskerville by Carnegie Publishing
Printed in the UK by The Alden Press, Oxford

British Library Cataloguing-in-Publication Data
A CIP catalogue record for this book is available from the British Library

ISBN 0-948789-84-0

CONTENTS

ACKNOWLEDGEMENTS

The author wishes to acknowledge the assistance of the *Evening Gazette*, Blackpool, particularly the Photographic and Library departments, and Malcolm Richardson of the South Fylde Line Users' Association in the preparation of this book.

INTRODUCTION

T HE FYLDE COAST phenomenon provides a fascinating footnote to the history of the Industrial Revolution in England. How a wind-blown peninsula, jutting defiantly into the Irish Sea, became the location of Europe's biggest tourist attraction remains a demographic mystery.

The Fylde is flat, forbidding and frost-flecked in winter; flat, fragrant and fertile in summer. Perched impertinently on the west Lancashire coast, it stretches from boisterous Blackpool, with its 12 million visitors a year, in the west to the ancient market town of Garstang in the east; from the fishing port of Fleetwood in the north to the Victorian and Edwardian gentility of Lytham St Annes in the south. Its landscape ranges from lush farmland dotted with copses, sloping eerily after the centuries-long onslaught of the south-westerly prevailing winds, to the treacherous marshland and muddy creeks of the Rivers Ribble and Wyre.

Almost all the Fylde's remarkable growth over the past century and a half can be attributed ultimately to one development – the railway. Until the railway's arrival, human habitation in the Fylde was piecemeal. The Romans came 2,000 years ago and built a road from their encampment at Ribchester through Kirkham, paralleling the present M55. But no-one seems sure why they should have done so, unless it was in search of a site for their legendary west-coast port. Several villages and hamlets grew up in the area, including Lytham, Marton, Layton, Warbreck, Bispham and Poulton.

By the end of the eighteenth century, Blackpool itself comprised little more than a string of inns and houses along the seafront, and from 1810 it developed slowly as a mainly middle-class watering place. With barely 700 residents, the town had a transport infrastructure that was minimal, particularly as far as links with the rest of Lancashire were concerned. Such a small community, isolated and inhospitable, certainly had no right to expect a railway line to be forged to its boundaries, which were marked out by moss, marsh and windmills.

About the only feature the Fylde had in its favour for the railway pioneers was its flatness, which was bound to endear it to Victorian engineers, with their abhorrence of hills and other topographical interruptions. In the event, the railway came to Blackpool almost as an afterthought, but it was an afterthought that helped lay the foundations of what has become Britain's fastest growing industry – tourism.

Chapter One

NOBLE INTENTS

SIR Peter Hesketh Fleetwood, politician, philanthropist, landowner and businessman, was a man out of his time: a romantic whose vision almost turned to tragedy. Throughout his life, he put service above self - and it came close to costing him his health, both physical and financial. Yet, his dream of a new community for the wage slaves of industrial Lancashire was realised, and his idealism - unlike that of more utopian social reformers - found a permanent memorial in the shape of a town and a railway.

Sir Peter was a man of complex and contradictory character. His idealistic vision left him ill, debilitated by anxiety and, ultimately, in relative penury. But the baronet had retained an impish sense of fun, often at his own expense. He enjoyed himself enormously by publicly manipulating the glass eye he had been forced to wear since losing the original during his undergraduate days at Oxford. He had classical good looks, with a firm, Roman nose, a strong, jutting chin and powerfully set lips. He was deeply religious and was passionately opposed to capital punishment, which in early Victorian times was still the penalty for more than 200 crimes. He was also a follower of the industrial reformer Robert Owen, whose factory at New Lanark was the scene of a non-profit making social experiment. From 1832–47 he represented Preston in Parliament, first as a Conservative before crossing the floor to become a Liberal. Though he was a classic example of an enlightened nineteenth-century gentleman-entrepreneur, however, his talents did not extend to accounts or ledgers. These he entrusted to others, often with dire results.

On the death of his father, in 1824, he had succeeded to the Rossall Hall estate on the northern edge of the Fylde as well as the Meols estate, which covered much of Southport. In 1831 he received royal permission to add

More than eight miles of track snaked around Fleetwood's docks when the railway and the port were at their peak. In this picture from July 1966, the giant track gauge of a quayside crane, loading a caravan on to a cargo vessel, dwarfs the 4ft 8½in of the railway. The parallel tracks could also be seen as a metaphor for the reciprocal development of the docks and railway in Fleetwood, a perfect example of integrated industrial activity involving two inextricably linked modes of transport.

the suffix 'Fleetwood' to his name in honour of his maternal forebears. The new lord of the manor was quick to realise that a port could profitably be established on the Wyre estuary - and that a new railway would be the ideal means of linking it with the outside world. New links were badly needed. Before the railway revolution, the main highway from Preston to the Fylde Coast was rutted and unpaved. In winter - or even a wet summer - it became impassable to the horse-drawn carts and stagecoaches which infrequently plied the route. On a good day, a coach from Manchester to Blackpool would leave Deansgate at dawn and arrive in the resort in the evening, with the Fylde leg of the journey alone taking three hours. The opening of the Clifton Turnpike, west of Preston, in 1781 im-

proved matters, but the coast's contacts with the outside world remained minimal.

With his imaginative - some would say visionary - intellect, Sir Peter realised the railway would change all that. While most lines in Britain served long-established communities, he was more akin to a North American railway pioneer - using the tracks to open up unexploited land and develop new settlements.

Though an idealist, Sir Peter was not a head-in-the-clouds dreamer, and he hoped his estates would share in the prosperity generated by his strong sense of public duty. Not only did he conceive a rail-linked port on his land but also an entire new town, more than a century before the concept was to become fashionable in places like Milton Keynes and, closer to home but less successfully, Skelmersdale. The town would be a fitting complement to the major port which he visualised as rivalling Liverpool in the provision of west-coast shipping services.

As High Sheriff of Lancashire, he witnessed the opening of the Liverpool to Manchester railway in 1830, and dreamed of bringing the downtrodden offspring of the Industrial Revolution to the haven of the Fylde's shores. His plans conveniently coincided with the recognition by a growing proportion of Lancashire's fast-expanding manufacturing community that the north of the county lacked adequate port and harbour provision. Inevitably, being Englishmen, they set up a committee, in 1830, to consider the matter. The committee investigated the competing claims of Lytham on the Ribble and Skippool creek and Wardley's creek on the Wyre. Also considered were Sir Peter's proposals for the Wyre estuary - not surprisingly, as he was a member of the committee. In the days long before the concept of corporate hospitality was devised, the lord of the manor took them on a boat trip down the Wyre to see the proposed site for themselves. Two days later, the committee met and plumped for the Rossall estate. Uppermost in members' minds must have been Sir Peter's pledge to develop an entirely new town that would be not just a port but also an elegant seaside watering place for Lancashire's burgeoning bourgeoisie.

The MP must have had considerable powers of persuasion,

however, for his estate did not seem at first sight the stuff of which industrial, domestic or even dockland dreams are made. In contemporary reports it is described as a vast, barren rabbit warren, with hardly any human habitation. It was on this wasteland that he founded his new town - which, in a rare concession to familial glory, was to be called Fleetwood. He engaged his friend Decimus Burton, a fashionable architect and student of John Nash, to mastermind the epic town planning project. Burton, who had gained national eminence through his designs for buildings around London's Regent's Park, marked out the first streets with a plough, steered by a farm labourer called Robert Banton, which gave a width and symmetry rare in northern towns. By April 1841, the North Euston Hotel, with its distinctive, curving façade, several smaller hotels, two churches, five streets and four rows of workmen's cottages had been completed. The population had reached almost 3,000.

Meanwhile, plans for the railway that would be Fleetwood's lifeline had begun in earnest in 1834. A group of merchants and civil leaders, including Sir Peter, Daniel Elletson of Preesall, Thomas Birley of Kirkham and Hugh Hornby of Ribby, published their Prospectus for the Preston and Wyre Railway. Colonel George Landmann was appointed surveyor and prepared a plan of the route which he suggested the new line should take. It would leave Preston from a station at Maudland Bank and pass through Lea, Salwick, Kirkham, Poulton, Thornton, the embryonic industrial town of Burn Naze (another Hesketh Fleetwood concept) and then on to Fleetwood. The most audacious part of the plan was to run the final part of the line over a specially constructed embankment across part of the Wyre estuary known as Cold Dubbs. It was a typically bold, not to say foolhardy, piece of nineteenth-century civil engineering. The Act of Parliament for the Preston and Wyre Railway received royal assent on 3 July 1835, authorising a capital of £130,000. The land for the venture was quickly bought by Frederick Kemp, a Hesketh Fleetwood estate manager and land agent, who – unlike his employer – was to prosper from the project.

Work began in 1836, with George Stephenson - the 'father of the railways' - and his brother Robert serving as engineers. After the contract for the Burn Naze embankment was let, large quantities of stone were brought from Heysham to form the huge construction and at the same time to protect some 5,000 acres which were to be reclaimed. By this time, it was confidently expected the River Wyre would be formidable competitor to the Mersey, but harbour dues would be only a fraction of Liverpool's. However, these hopes soon began to grow sour. By the beginning of 1839, there were 100 houses in Fleetwood but still no railway. Eminent engineer Joseph Locke, of the Grand Union Railway, was

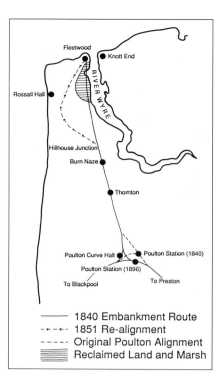

1840 Embankment Route
1851 Re-alignment
Original Poulton Alignment
Reclaimed Land and Marsh

Preston and Wyre Railway. This map shows the changing route of the Preston and Wyre Railway in the nineteenth century. The precarious original route across the Wyre to Fleetwood was abandoned when the sounder but more circuitous line to the west opened in 1851. The abandonment of the problem-prone embankment enabled a tract of land on the inner side of the piling to be reclaimed for development. To the south, the original route through Poulton was replaced by a new triangular configuration between 1896 and 1899 after an accident which claimed three lives.

called in to report on the unfinished work. He estimated the cost of the embankment to be far higher than budgeted for, and forecast that the eventual cost of the whole line would be approaching £300,000 - more than double the amount authorised by the Act. At one point, 300 labourers and 45 horses were working round the clock on the embankment in the face of powerful and destructive tides. The delays in the construction of the embankment led to its substitution for part of the distance by a timber trestle, intended only as a temporary measure.

By now, though, the soaring costs of the railway were beginning to put a strain on Sir Peter's substantial resources. After the

Locke report, Sir Peter personally undertook responsibility for completion of the line. He sold land in Preston, North Meols and Blackpool to help meet his expenses. (His Blackpool land sales provided an interesting historical footnote. In his haste to raise money, he sold to speculative builders who developed the resort in a haphazard way, far removed from the ordered development he would have ensured if the land had remained in his hands.) His problems were compounded early in 1840 when one of the arches of the Maudland viaduct at Preston – the only other major piece of engineering work on the line – collapsed as it was nearing completion. Eleven workmen died.

None of this augured well for the future of the line, but Sir Peter and his fellow directors were able to forget the gloom, at least temporarily, during the opening ceremony on 15 July 1840. Waved off by thousands of well-wishers in Fleetwood, a decorated double-headed train took the guests, including civic leaders and George Stephenson, to Preston and back on the single-track line. Huge crowds turned out *en route*. The return journey took exactly an hour, and was followed by a lavish lunch, a short sea trip and, in the evening, a grand ball. The celebrations were marred only by the death of a reveller who slipped from a carriage on to the track.

To the relief of shareholders, passenger projections had greatly under-estimated the numbers who would use the line.

The public service started the day after the official opening, and 20,000 passengers were carried in the first month - more than the expected annual volume. In the six summer months of 1841, the total was 107,920. Three trains operated daily on weekdays in each direction. Fares were: first class, 4s. 6d.; second, 3s.; third, 2s. The only intermediate stations on the 19½-mile line were at Kirkham and Poulton.

Travel to Fleetwood must have been a daunting experience for passengers from inland, unfamiliar with the estuary. At high tide, the water extended for about a ¾ mile on either side of the banking and waves would occasionally wash over it. Trains crossed cautiously, although the proprietors insisted there was no danger. Perhaps a bigger threat to safety were the conditions in which passengers were carried. Initially, conditions on the P & W were, by early Victorian standards, reasonably comfortable. As the bigger and less scrupulous railway companies homed in on the line for excursion purposes, however, the state of the rolling stock began to deteriorate dramatically. The railway companies' enthusiasm for transporting the working classes across the country, at half the normal fare, was not usually an act of altruism. Excursion trains were highly profitable, especially on Sundays when there was plenty of spare rolling stock, parked idly in sidings. The standard stock for a cut-price excursion was an open cattle truck (swept out, of course). If you were lucky, benches would be fitted; if not, simple cross-bars to which the hapless passenger had to cling grimly. The trucks were loose-coupled, and the resulting jolts could easily cause broken limbs. On a wet day, conditions were dire, although in sunshine it could be a pleasant, if hazardous, journey.

However, it was a much more sedate source that was to provide the P & W with much of its early revenue. The Sunday school movement was rapidly expanding in central and east Lancashire, and its teachers were always looking out for healthy, wholesome activities for their charges. Trips to the seaside fitted the bill admirably. One day in 1842, a delegation of Sunday school staff from Preston arrived at the railway office in Fleetwood with an unusual proposition. The result, on 3 July, was an excursion for more than 2,000 hymn-singing pupils and teachers from Preston - one of the first cheap rail trips in Britain. It was the forerunner of many similar ventures to Fleetwood. On one such excursion, the vicar, unable to find a seat elsewhere, travelled with his flock in an open wagon and later told his bishop he had never enjoyed a railway journey so much. In 1848, 2,000 Prestonians joined the Poor People's Annual Summer Excursion to the port, at 6d. a head. Initially, the excursions were organised with typical high-minded paternalism, to supplant 'debasing and degrading habits by innocent and healthful recreation'. These noble objectives, however, would soon be supplanted by less idealistic aims.

Returns for shareholders, though, were still slow to arrive. Perhaps one of Fleetwood's problems - not uncommon during the Industrial Revolution - was that it was over-ambitious. Its pioneers saw the Preston-Wyre link as part of a grand Anglo-Scottish trunk route, linking London to Glasgow. And so it was ... briefly. Passengers travelled from London to Fleetwood, then by steamer to Ardrossan before completing the journey with another, short train trip to Glasgow. The journey took 27 hours. On 20 September 1847, Queen Victoria, Prince Albert, the Prince of Wales and the Princess Royal landed at Fleetwood *en route* from the Western Isles to London. The Queen, who had made Sir Peter a baronet in her first honours list in 1838, presented him with her white kid gloves and a quill pen. A year earlier Thomas Cook had organised his first excursion to Scotland by the same route. But its glory was to be short-lived. Many railway engineers had been openly sceptical about the possibility of pushing a line over the formidably steep Shap Fell in Cumbria and of developing a locomotive sufficiently powerful to haul a train over it. Their scepticism was unwarranted. The west-coast main line was completed by the Caledonian Railway in 1848, rendering the Fleetwood route obsolete for London-Scottish traffic. It was a body blow for the P & W, a railway which had begun life with the loftiest of expectations. So large were the expected takings that

Opposite:
A Victorian vista ... a panoramic view of the departure of Queen Victoria, her consort Prince Albert and the royal children from Fleetwood by the artist John Eastham. In September 1847, the royal party had landed at the port en route from the Western Isles to London. Crowds of crinolined ladies and top-hatted gentlemen line the embankment opposite the royal train, hauled by a Preston and Wyre Railway 0-6-0 locomotive. The work is dedicated to 'Sir P.H. Fleetwood, Bart, the Founder of that Town and Port', who is portrayed in bewhiskered grandeur, surrounded by laurel leaves, at the base of the picture. An estimated 50,000 people saw the arrival of the royal yacht and its accompanying squadron.

the company equipped its Fleetwood office with a set of scales and a copper shovel - to weigh the revenue. The shovel ended its days, more prosaically, fuelling the office fire. After only a handful of years, the venture seemed on the verge of oblivion. The line was frequently criticised in the railway press for failing to publish details of its affairs. Its shares were changing hands for a fraction of their proper price. Investors were still muttering about the absence of dividends. The entire railway, harbour and town scheme ground to a halt. When the harbour work came to a standstill, the railway company could not pay interest on borrowed capital, and a new share issue failed. Sir Peter's personal position worsened. He had ploughed much of his own fortune into the project, and in 1844 he sold Rossall Hall for use as a school - it remains one of Britain's leading public schools. Cruelly, special trains were run to the sale of the hall's contents along the line that he had created and which had led to his financial downfall. Eventually a committee of investigation was formed. It concluded that the enterprise was fundamentally sound but said the line should be managed by local directors. The London directors resigned and a local board was appointed under the chairmanship of the Rochdale banker, Clement Royds. Sir Peter,

the begetter of Fleetwood, re-tired to the South, where he was to spend the rest of his life. Thankfully free of the physical and financial frenzy of the rail-way project, his health began to rally.

The line's fortunes began to im-prove under the new regime and dividends materialised. Wayside halts were opened at Lea Road, Salwick, Weeton and Ramper (Thornton), though the last two closed soon after. In 1846-7 the main line was doubled between Preston and Burn Naze, where the timber trestle was causing increasing alarm among passen-gers and the line's engineers. To avoid the expense of doubling the two-mile embankment line, a link following the shore to the west was planned. This opened on 13 February 1851, after which the foundations of the banking developed further trouble and it was finally abandoned. Many P & W veterans breathed a deep sigh of relief. It had been – literally – a pile of problems. However, it was to be another 30 years before the original Fleetwood terminus was replaced. In 1883, an impressive £120,000 new station, with an all-over roof and attractive floral displays, was opened in the port, next to the steamer berths. The former Dock Street terminus was closed. Another new station was opened, at Wyre Dock, in 1885.

The development of the rail-way and of Fleetwood's maritime connections were indissolubly linked from the beginning. It was to become a classic example of integrated industrial activity, with docks and rail lines meshing intricately to help create the port's prosperity. Even before the railway had opened, the P & W company had bought a steamer which plied between Fleetwood and Bardsea, near Ulverston. A company was formed to improve shipping facilities at Fleetwood and was given power by the Pre-ston and Wyre Dock Act of 5 May 1837 to build docks with author-ised capital of £100,000. A plan for the new dock was produced by Colonel Landmann in 1836 but no progress was made. Three years later, the dock and railway companies were amalgamated by Act of Parliament. Despite the snail's-pace progress of the docks, on 7 October 1841 Sir Peter reported that steamer services were operating to the Isle of Man, Whitehaven, Belfast and Ardros-san. The link with Douglas was the first forged on 15 August 1840 when the paddle steamer *James Dennistoun* set out to make the 60-mile, seven-hour trip for just three shillings.

Fleetwood developed as a packet station despite the fact that the expected trade from overseas proved disappointing. The outbreak of the American Civil War in 1861 savaged the cot-ton trade. However, the local trade provided some compensa-tion. The 15-mile hop across Morecambe Bay from Fleetwood to Barrow proved one of the most popular passenger routes, pro-viding a gateway to the Lake Dis-trict. By contrast, travellers going overland faced a gruelling rail-way journey via Preston and Carnforth. The quality of the 'rolling stock' used by the North

Lancashire Steam Navigation Company probably exceeded that of the rail lines which served it. Two distinguished steamers, *Her Majesty* and *Royal Consort*, operated the Ardrossan run while *Princess Alice* and *Prince of Wales* served Belfast.

The main activity centred on the nightly departure for Belfast at 10.45 p.m. The operators wasted no time in moving passengers from train to boat. The 5.30 p.m. from Euston did not arrive until 10.25 p.m. while the Lancashire-Yorkshire express from Leeds and Manchester arrived with just seven minutes to spare. These were the sort of margins that left little room for error. It was a slick, sophisticated operation which relied on clockwork precision and almost military-style logistical planning, aided by the fact that the berths lay directly alongside the station.

Meanwhile, though, there had been a 30-year hiatus in developing the long dreamed-of docks. Work did not begin until 1869 – three years after Sir Peter's death – and was soon abandoned after some progress had been made. In 1871 the Lancashire and Yorkshire Railway obtained powers to complete the work. The company first bought 600 acres of the Fleetwood estate and appointed John Hawkshaw as chief engineer. A tender of about £130,000 was accepted for the main work, but the actual cost was £303,057 – paralleling, with uncanny closeness, the overshoot on the Preston-Wyre rail line. The dock was opened on 8 October 1877, covering 10 acres and with 2,700ft of quay space. More than eight miles of railway track surrounded the dock. To handle imports of grain more efficiently, a giant elevator was built on the east side of the dock. It could unload grain cargoes at the rate of 120 tons per hour.

Trade through the Wyre dock was varied, including iron ore, pig iron, potatoes, wood pulp and china clay from Cornwall. But it was the fishing industry that was to prove the staple of Fleetwood's growing prosperity. By the end of the century, annual fish tonnage exceeded 5,000; in 1905 it was 13,772; and in 1909, 50,995. By then it had become clear that the fish trade needed new facilities, and it was decided to convert part of the existing timber 'pond' into a separate fish dock. It was a prescient decision. The number of sailing smacks based in the port had jumped from 32 in 1862 to 84 when Wyre dock was opened, and, by the outbreak of World War One, more than 100 steam trawlers were sailing from the port. It was hoped flourishing Fleetwood would rival Grimsby for dominance in the fishing industry. The layout of the rail tracks was designed to make the transfer of goods from trawler to train as streamlined as possible. Ventilated vans used for carrying the fish were all fitted with connecting pipes so they could be kept working on express trains.

It was all a far cry from the precarious origins of the Preston and Wyre Railway, Harbour and Dock Company. As the inevitable amalgamation and acquisitions of smaller railway companies proceeded apace throughout the nineteenth century, the P & W had merged with the Manchester and Leeds Railway from 3 August 1846 but was not finally dissolved until 1 July 1888 under an Act dated 7 August of that year. Section 68 ruled that a joint committee be appointed by the London and North Western Railway and the L & Y to manage the lines. The Act merely formalised a leasing arrangement by the L & Y and LNWR which had existed for almost forty years, though the P & W would no longer be operated as a separate entity. The L & Y was the senior partner, with two-thirds of the joint arrangement, and the LNWR one third.

This unusual partnership, and the involvement of mighty Westminster in the workings of the railway to the Wyre, served to highlight the tortuous and sometimes caustic relationship between the railway companies and Parliament. Though the middle decades of the nineteenth century were widely held to be the heyday of *laissez faire* economics, government regulation of railways began as early as 1840 - the year Sir Peter's railway opened. The railway interests, through sympathetic MPs and peers, fought a rear-guard action against moves to extend the powers of the Railway Commissioners. However, Sir Edward Ryan, the Commissioner of Railways from 1846-51 and a former Chief Justice of Bengal, was not a man to be intimidated. He made the commissioners' presence felt both through comments on legislation and, occasionally, through direct pressure on parties interested in the myriad railway Bills passed through Parliament. For instance, in the 1849 Bill to give the L & Y and LNWR their leasing powers on the P & W, the commissioners objected to clauses relating to proposed tolls, and Sir Edward won a pledge that they would be withdrawn. By the time the Fylde's first railway company was officially wound up 39 years later, it had enjoyed a chequered but ultimately charmed existence. However, this was due, almost by accident, to an obscure settlement seven miles down the coast.

Chapter Two

BLACKPOOL AND LYTHAM

BLACKPOOL was already developing as a minor seaside resort by the end of the eighteenth century, but the arrival of the railway was instrumental in transforming it into Europe's busiest holiday centre. The town takes its name from a peaty coloured 'pool', or stream, which formerly drained into the sea somewhere near Foxhall. A few visitors came here even when it was only a fishing hamlet, to enjoy the bracing air and fresh breezes, but at the beginning of the nineteenth century it was still a comparatively small and unknown place. By the time the railway reached Fleetwood, in 1840, the population of Blackpool was still only about 2000, less than half the size of its upstart northern neighbour. But there were clear signs that its prosperity was rapidly increasing, and that runaway growth was under way.

The most significant sign was the number of passengers who, forsaking the attractions of the growing seaside resort of Fleetwood, would leave the train at Poulton and travel on to Blackpool by road. Perhaps 'road' is too generous a description of the bumpy, four-mile lane that wound its way to the resort, taking half an hour to negotiate. Many of the horse-buses which met passengers at Poulton were owned by the proprietors of the handful of hotels that had grown up in Blackpool. The hoteliers would assail disembarking passengers with shouted details of their tariffs. It was the start of a long tradition of touting for custom at railway stations, which survived until trains ceased to be the main means of travel to Blackpool and more sophisticated inducements had to be deployed. According to one story, perhaps apocryphal, the impetus for a railway connection to Blackpool came from a director of the Preston and Wyre Railway who had to complete his journey to Blackpool on a wagonette squashed between a party of large and vocal trippers from Yorkshire.

As in Fleetwood's case, however, a major driving force in the extension of the railway to Blackpool was a local landowner. Thomas Clifton owned the Layton estate on the east side of town, through which any rail link to Blackpool would have to pass. In June 1842 he bought the manorial rights of Blackpool for less than £500 from Sir Peter Hesketh Fleetwood, who was desperately seeking finance to keep the Preston and Wyre solvent. In December 1843 Clifton paid £4,980 for a large chunk of the old Forshaw estate, including a strip of land that ran from Layton Hall to the seafront, near the site of the present North Pier. It was this that provided the corridor along which the railway would come to Blackpool. Clifton laid a new road to the promenade, ending in a large and imposing square – Talbot Square.

At a meeting on 30 September 1844, meanwhile, proposals were put forward for branches of the Preston and Wyre Railway from Poulton to Blackpool and Kirkham to Lytham. An Act was obtained less than a year later. A deal was struck with Thomas Clifton to allow the Blackpool branch to run roughly parallel with Talbot Road. The station was to be sited on the brow of a low hill opposite the Talbot Hotel: it could have been located nearer the seafront but the rising land would have made it difficult for departing locomotives pulling tripper-packed excursions. The spoil from the excavation work for the station was used to fill in a cleft in the seafront and remove this obstacle to the extension of the promenade. It was an example of co-operation between the resort and the railway that was not always continued, as future relations between the two sides grew increasingly fractious. The single-line branch was built in just four months. As the line approached Blackpool, the contractor – a Mr Jardine – laid a set of rails from the station to the seafront, where the wagon loads of spoil were tipped into the cleft and the empty trucks drawn back up the hill by horses.

Celebrated by a flag-festooned special train 24 hours earlier, the line opened to the public on 29 April 1846. Thomas Clifton and the Preston and Wyre Railway Board soon realised they had made a shrewd investment. The nascent resort quickly proved to be a more popular draw than Fleetwood and droves of passengers thronged the new terminus in Talbot Road.

Though one of the more handsome pieces of architecture in the town, with its Roman Ionic stone portico, the building boasted an interior that was distinctly spartan, and the administration of the station was casual. The *Preston Guardian*, the nearest thing to a local newspaper until the arrival of the *Blackpool Herald* in 1855 and the *Blackpool Gazette* in 1873, described the resort as the Brighton of the North. This, however, applied to its popularity rather than its architecture or town planning – and popular it was.

As with Fleetwood, excursion trade proved the biggest money-earner. With the Industrial Revolution gathering pace, the inhabitants of the mill country of east Lancashire and Yorkshire yearned for the fresh air and frolics of the Fylde, away from the soot-blackened factories, twelve-hour shifts and back-to-back terrace housing of their home towns.

In 1846, to celebrate the repeal of the Corn Laws, the entire 1,300-strong workforce of the enlightened entrepreneur Richard Cobden piled into trains at Chorley one sunny morning in July, Blackpool-bound, to be followed later the same month by a Sunday school party of 4,200 children and parents on a day's outing.

An 1848 excursion from Oldham cost just one shilling for ladies, and sixpence more for gentlemen . . . but the concession was withdrawn because it was suspected that men were masquerading as women to obtain the cheaper fare. But the biggest excursion of all came on 1 June 1849, when every carriage that was not needed for the normal Sunday service was commandeered from stations across east Lancashire. One train left Rochdale, calling at Heywood and Bury, by which time it consisted of no fewer than 55 coaches. At Bolton it joined up with another, similar-sized train

from Ashton, Stalybridge and Oldham. With three other trains from Manchester and Bolton the extraordinary excursion set off for Blackpool and Fleetwood in convoy. It was probably the first – and certainly the greatest – rail excursion of its kind, with more that 10,000 people in almost 200 carriages and trucks being whisked through the fields of the Fylde to the coast. Thousands of spectators gathered to watch the remarkable procession. The era of the great excursion had arrived – and so had Blackpool.

But there was activity at the other end of the coast, too. Like Blackpool, Lytham existed before the end of the eighteenth century as a sea-bathing resort. Unlike its brash neighbour, however, it had for centuries been a base for fishermen in the Ribble estuary and Irish Sea. A mile to the east lay Lytham Pool, where ships with cargoes for Preston often unloaded into smaller vessels. Attempts to promote a railway were made in 1837 and 1840. The Squire of Lytham, Thomas Joseph Clifton, was less than enthusiastic about the idea. However, he was 'willing to admit its advantages to the village'. He withdrew his objections when it was pointed out that the line would skirt his estate without serious encroachment on to his farms, but he observed: 'I suggest . . . the terminus should be at a distance from any building ground for houses as may be consistent with its general convenience as no-one would like to be in the immediate neighbourhood of a railroad'.

But it was the construction of a small dock at Lytham that seems to have provided the necessary impetus for development of the railway. Work on the 4¾-mile single line from Kirkham began at the end of July 1845, at a cost of £4,000 per mile. It opened two months ahead of the Blackpool branch – on 17 February 1846. A mile west of Kirkham, the branch left the main line and about a mile from the terminus a short spur diverged to serve Lytham Dock. The station at Lytham was similar to the one in Talbot Road, with an all-over roof 140ft long and 53ft wide, designed by the architect R. B. Rampling. The centre-piece was an imposing, octagonal booking hall. Two intermediate stations were opened, Moss Side and Wray Green (as it was then spelt: it acquired the present day spelling of Wrea Green in 1875). Ten years earlier a station had been opened at Warton for Lytham Dock but closed on 1 May 1874.

A platform at Lytham Junction, where the branch left the main line west of Kirkham, had closed in November 1853. However, through coaches continued to be attached to, and uncoupled from, main line trains at the junction until 1874. In that year a new line was opened which cut off the original junction – which was at a very sharp angle – and ran more directly between Wrea Green and Kirkham. The old line then became a siding and Lytham Junction was no more.

By the middle of the nineteenth century, the Fylde was traversed by railways to the north, south and east. What it lacked was a western link – a coastal route connecting Blackpool with the communities of South Fylde. Blackpool's popularity had continued to grow apace. In 1865–66 the Blackpool branch was converted to double track at a cost of £24,000 and, in 1867, a station was opened at Bispham (renamed Layton in July 1938), 1½ miles from the resort. But the great railway development of the decade was the construction of the coastal route. On 17 May 1861 an Act was passed authorising £45,000 capital for a line between Blackpool and Lytham. The estimated cost of the 7½-mile single line was £30,000. Work on the Blackpool and Lytham Railway was completed by autumn 1862, but as winter traffic was unlikely to be profitable, the opening was delayed until 6 April the following year – seven weeks before Blackpool's first pier was inaugurated. At first there was only one intermediate station, at South Shore, two miles from central Blackpool.

The resort of St Annes did not yet exist. Nevertheless, the line carried 35,000 passengers in its first three months. In April 1865, a station opened at Stony Hill (near Squires Gate) but it disappeared from the timetable seven years later. In November 1873 a station was opened at Cross Slack, 4½ miles south of Blackpool, but this too was short lived; it closed in 1875. In the same year, however, a replacement was opened at St Annes, the new town which was to be founded nearby.

There was also a station at Ansdell, which opened in 1872.

The Blackpool and Lytham led a dangerous life. Bisecting the sandhills between the two destinations, it survived several floods, and at one point the sea washed away the embankment behind the Manchester Hotel in Blackpool. But it seems to have held its customers in higher regard than the Preston and Wyre Railway. According to one contemporary newspaper report, the width of the third-class carriages was such that 'passengers can sit without the usual action of grinding their knees against those of fellow passengers sitting opposite, and when a man is weary of sitting he may stretch himself without the risk of smashing his hat against the roof. In every way the carriages contrast favourably with the filthy prison vans in ordinary use'.

The company owned two locomotives, both 2-2-2 tanks. The only one in use at the opening was *The Little Queen*, built for the Great Exhibition of 1851 and two years later bought by the St Helens Railway Co. When it was eventually acquired by the Blackpool and Lytham, it cost the queenly sum of £750. A report in the *Preston Guardian* spoke of 'two new and powerful engines in the course of construction for the company' by Sharp Stewart and Co. of Manchester. Only one was acquired, however, a saddle tank appropriately called *The King*, at a cost of £1,440.

The Blackpool and Lytham may have had impressive rolling stock; what it lacked was any physical connection to the rest of the nation's network. The station at Lytham was several hundred yards from the Preston and Wyre terminus, and the station at Hound's Hall, Blackpool, about half a mile from Talbot Road. When the new Lytham terminus had been built, *The Little Queen* had to be physically hauled from one station to the other. This remarkable feat was accomplished by a team of 17 horses which dragged the locomotive along the line of Westby Street. After the slowest journey of its life, pulled a few yards at a time over a laboriously laid pathway of railway sleepers, the engine eventually arrived safely at its destination.

By 1871, however, the line was faced with mounting financial problems, and directors sold out to the L & Y and LNWR, as joint proprietors of the Preston and Wyre Railway, on 1 July. The Act which provided for the absorption of the Blackpool and Lytham also authorised a new connection line to the Preston and Wyre at Lytham, making a direct link to Preston. It cost £135,000 to make the connection and double the entire length of track from Kirkham to Blackpool. The original terminus at Lytham was closed, becoming a goods station, and the through line opened on 1 July 1874. The Blackpool and Lytham Co.'s northern terminus, Hound's Hill, was renamed Blackpool Central in 1878. The original Blackpool station had already been redesignated Blackpool (Talbot Road).

It was not all hustle and bustle

on the Lytham branch, however. Along the line lay tranquil backwaters which flitted past the carriage windows as the tourists' trains sped by. Such a station was Moss Side near Lytham. In her classic book *Fylde Folk: Moss or Sand*, the late Kathleen Eyre, doyenne of local historians, paints an elegiac picture of life inside the Moss Side station house in the last century. Her hero is 'Owd Jem' Fisher, resplendent in blue uniform piped with red, who combined the offices of stationmaster, booking clerk, porter and lamplighter at the postcard-pretty rural halt.

Passengers passed through turnstile gates to the booking office, converted from the station house porch, which was one step below the platform level.

'At the tapping of a coin, Jem opened the living room door and, with a practised movement, lowered a board hinged to the wall to form a counter.'

Jem apparently liked to chat to his customers but the sudden slamming of the living room door would remind him that his wife, Mag, disapproved of this friendly banter. But Mag shared her husband's passion for cleanliness, and if Moss Side was not the busiest station on the line, it was one of the neatest.

Traffic volumes varied. The day began with the arrival of the early morning milk train at 6.15 a.m. Farmers sold their milk to a St Annes dairy, bringing their produce twice daily to the station in floats. Jem - now donning his porter's cap - hoisted the cans into the guard's van before joining his family for breakfast.

During the week few passengers boarded the morning trains for Blackpool and Preston, but on visiting days at Moss Side Hospital (now closed), the station came into its own. On Saturdays, too, hordes of farmers would board the 8.50 a.m. Market Special to Preston. In the evening, Jem underwent a further metamorphosis into the station lamplighter, igniting the tall pedestal oil lamps for the long night.

It would never occur to him, writes Miss Eyre, that the little station would one day be closed and quietly overgrown - 'and that trains would thunder through, never stopping, as though they had forgotten all about a place called Moss Side.' The book was first published in 1970. Happily since then, a new station has risen from the weed-clogged remnants of the original halt. There is no Jem - it is unmanned - but both he and Miss Eyre would be comforted to know that the moss has not been allowed to take hold on Moss Side.

In many ways, of course, the station was untypical, For much of its length, the Blackpool and Lytham branch was predominantly an urban and suburban line with urban objectives. The coastal route to Blackpool was the single most important railway development in the Fylde in the second half of the nineteenth century. Not only did it help bring into being the new town of St Annes, it also opened up another holiday artery to Blackpool - albeit one just as circuitous as the original line through

Poulton. This pattern of railway development was to shape the resort's geography right up to the present day, and the council would spend a century trying to remove the railway from prime sites in the centre of the town.

Chapter Three

EXPANSION: 1870-1914

AFTER three decades of headlong growth from 1840, the Fylde's railway operators could have been forgiven for resting on their laurels and consolidating their achievements. But that was not Blackpool's way. The period up the outbreak of World War One was marked by further explosive expansion that finally established the resort's seven golden miles as the most alluring holiday destination in the country – for the working man and his family at least.

At the same time, Blackpool's entertainment attractions, many of which still dominate the seaside skyline, were taking shape through the town's unprecedented partnership between public and private enterprise. Tens of thousands of Wakes Weeks trippers from the textile towns of east Lancashire and Yorkshire flocked to the resort. An imposing new promenade was laid, the palatial Winter Gardens complex built, electric street lighting pioneered and, on 29 September 1885, the historic electric tramway system opened. A rash of theatres made their entrances, the ill-fated Big Wheel turned for the first time and, at Whitsuntide 1894, the town's most famous landmark, the Tower, was officially opened. Meanwhile, legions of lodging houses were springing up, mainly around the two rail termini, to cater for the army of trippers seeking cheap, comfortable accommodation. One of the biggest attractions of the resort, though, was that it claimed to have the longest unbroken stretch of beach in the North West.

The relationship between the railway and the resort was symbiotic. Each depended on the other. Expansion of the railway fuelled development in the resort, which by 1900 had a population approaching 50,000, and this in turn stimulated still more railway enterprise. Yet the reciprocal relationship was often uneasy. Under the joint ownership arrangement whereby the Lancashire and Yorkshire and the LNWR ran the Preston and Wyre lines, the L & Y had a two-thirds share of the new set-up. With its near monopoly of services in east Lancashire, the company had a virtual stranglehold on the resort's rail links. Critics accused the company of lack of enterprise and of inhibiting Blackpool's development, and there is a brittleness in the railway's relations with the civic authorities which remains to this day.

There was no evidence, however, of a lack of entrepreneurial flair in the final quarter of the nineteenth century. To cope with the increasing railway traffic, a contract for quadrupling the track from Preston to Kirkham was let to Thomas Riley for £140,000 in March 1888. The four-track layout opened the following year. At the same time, a new station was built at Kirkham and a double-track diversion constructed at Poulton for Blackpool traffic. This was designed to ease the problems caused by the tight curve at Poulton, where in July 1893 a Blackpool-Stockport train left the rails, killing three people and injuring 36. At the inquest the railway companies were accused of culpable negligence, and the inspecting officer urged no delay in starting the improvements. The deviation scheme, including about $2\frac{1}{2}$ miles of new line and a new Poulton station, was opened on 5 April 1896. The original station and a short length of track beyond the Poulton level crossing became a goods terminal, and su-

perfluous portions of the original main line and branch line were abandoned. The work, which eased the passage to Blackpool at the expense of the journey to Fleetwood, underlined the changing relative importance of the two resorts. A direct Blackpool-Fleetwood curve was laid in 1899, making a triangular configuration, but this is now long abandoned - reclaimed by weeds and wild flowers.

Lesser developments included the opening, in 1870 and 1865, respectively, of stations at Singleton and Cleveleys, though the latter was some two miles from the small resort after which it was optimistically named. On 1 April 1905 it became, more realistically, Thornton for Cleveleys, and was replaced by a new station 20 years later. Halts at Poulton curve and Burn Naze were opened on 1 February 1909 and 12 October 1908 respectively, in connection with a railmotor service which operated from Blackpool to Fleetwood.

In Blackpool, meanwhile, the former P & W terminus in Talbot Road was completely rebuilt and enlarged. Work began in 1896 and the new platforms saw their first passengers at Whitsuntide the following year. When it was finally completed in spring 1898, the main platforms had a total length of 3,600 feet and the excursion platforms (site of the present Blackpool North station) of 6,300 feet.

But still there was pressure from civic leaders on the Fylde coast for yet more improvements. The L & Y and LNWR said they

The wraith of an old railway cuts across from Breck Road, Poulton, towards Thornton. This was the alignment of the original Preston-Fleetwood railway, which skirted Poulton-le-Fylde to the north-east. The picture shows the Breck Road level crossing in the background. A fatal accident in 1893 prompted a major re-routing of the line, isolating the 1840 station, though the sidings remained in use. For a time, Poulton had the luxury of no fewer than three stations, with a halt being open on a new curve connecting the Blackpool and Fleetwood lines.

would build new lines when they became necessary. Barely a decade later, however, they were compelled to act by force of circumstance. Blackpool traffic had grown so fast by 1895 that a direct route to the resort – virtually as the crow flies from Preston – became a necessity. The solution was to build the Fylde's third and last route from Kirkham, cutting a swathe through the countryside east of Blackpool and running almost directly into the town centre. On 20 July 1896 the two companies obtained the necessary Act, which also authorised the widening of the former Blackpool and Lytham Railway from South Shore to Central stations. Known as the New Line or Marton Line, it ran 6¾ miles from Kirkham North junction to Blackpool Central, joining the coast line about 300 yards north of South Shore station. The line,

crossing 17 bridges, opened for goods traffic on 21 April 1903 and for passengers on 30 May. Meanwhile, the railway companies unveiled another bold piece of engineering: a single-line flyover connecting the Blackpool track from the Lytham direction with the north side of the main line at Kirkham. The only station on the New Line was at Waterloo Road, at the junction with the coast line close to South Shore. On 14 July 1916 it was logically converted into a junction station by the provision of an island platform serving the coast line, and the older South Shore station was closed. Waterloo Road was renamed Blackpool South on 17 March 1932.

The shift in Blackpool's centre of gravity from north to south was continued by the rebuilding of Central station, which began in 1899. The new station, with

Right – Looking more like a cottage than a railway building, with its half-timbered walls, the old St Annes Station is pictured at the turn of the century, A horse and carriage add even more atmosphere to this evocative scene.

Below – This was the original gateway to the Golden Mile. The Ionic-style Talbot Road Station was built in 1846 before being demolished 50 years later to make way for a vastly enlarged building, which opened in spring 1898. This picture is believed to have been taken shortly before the closure of the old station.

Holiday-makers strolling along Blackpool promenade in spring 1911 could have been forgiven for performing a startled double-take as a steam-shrouded locomotive thundered past at the head of a column of trucks on a prom widening project. This smoke-stained vision was the Sands Express, which for the first and only time brought steam to the seafront in Blackpool. The 1903 loco Reliance (pictured near the Clifton Hotel) was involved in an accident when the embankment at the Metropole subsided, but it was back at work within an hour. The Sands Express steamed its last in the middle of May 1911.

almost 9,000 feet of regular and excursion platforms, was completed for Easter 1901, and the widening from South Shore to Central two years later.

Halts were opened at Gillett's crossing, near the present St Annes Old Links golf course, and Burlington Road on 1 October 1913, and a railmotor service introduced between Blackpool Central and Lytham. The halts closed exactly two years later but reopened after the end of World War One. They finally closed a week into World War Two, though Burlington Road is now the site of the new Blackpool Pleasure Beach station.

Rail traffic was not all one way, however. By the middle of the nineteenth century, the Fylde coast had become a popular dormitory area for Manchester-based businessmen. Its health-giving properties made it the ideal environment for industrialists fleeing the smog of Manchester every evening and weekend. Many of these entrepreneurs retired to Blackpool or, later, St Annes, and found themselves with time - and money - on their hands. Often they chose to invest it in the rising resorts, providing much of the motive force behind their development.

But the Manchester-Fylde coast commuters could not be expected to mingle with the hordes of holiday-makers, many of whom were their employees. Their solution was to form consortia to run so called Club Carriages between Blackpool Central and Manchester. Membership of the club was restricted to 50 first-class ticket holders, who paid an annual fee for the privilege. Carriages became increasingly opulent, generally being hauled each evening by the

Opposite:
It was the tramway equivalent of its naval contemporary and namesake, HMS Dreadnought. Blackpool's Dreadnought trams were unique to the resort, with their double staircases at each end of the open-top vehicles. This is the only survivor of the fleet, tramcar no. 59, built in 1902, recovered from undignified retirement at the back of a tram shed in 1959, and lovingly restored for the 75th anniversary of the tramway the following year. No. 59 was one of the stars of the centenary celebrations in 1985, when it returned from the National Tramway Museum at Crich to grace the anniversary procession.

5.10 p.m. and 5.55 p.m. expresses. Each had a uniformed attendant-cum-valet. A less well known train for businessmen in east Lancashire ran non-stop from Lytham to Rose Grove, near Burnley. Club members were bound by strict rules. Each had his own seat and dire penalties threatened anyone who had the temerity to open a window in an attempt to ventilate the fog of cigar smoke inside the special saloon. But members received good value for their three guinea subscription. The trip between Manchester and Lytham could be completed in an hour – faster than present-day timings – while members relaxed in leather upholstered armchairs.

If the Club Carriages' commuters were the aristocrats among railway passengers, there was another railway aristocrat-in-the-making working quietly away at

the Blackpool Central motive power depot at the turn of the century. The young Nigel Gresley was learning his trade as running shed foreman at the Central shed as part of his training. As Sir Nigel Gresley, he went on to become one of the world's legendary locomotive designers, his famous Streamliners – most notably the *Mallard* – consistently breaking rail speed records.

World war put a temporary break on Blackpool's expansion in 1914, but after the Armistice millions of war-weary men and women were ready to forget the horrors of the conflict amid the good natured vulgarity and ozone laden air of the Fylde coast.

Chapter Four

THE PILLING PIG

ONE of the smallest and most eccentric adjuncts to the North West rail network blazed an unassuming trail across the desolate mossland of the Fylde's northern fringe. The Garstang and Knott End Railway, known affectionately as the Pilling Pig, was a resolutely rural line, in stark contrast to the busy tourist routes of Blackpool. In scenes straight out of a story by the Rev. W. Awdry, 0-6-0 tank engines snorted and grunted across the aptly named line, pulling trains laden with farm produce. But the idiosyncratic branch led a hand-to-mouth existence, with financial crises continually on the horizon.

Garstang station on the Lancaster and Preston Junction Railway lay about 1¾ miles from the town after which it was named. To the west lay an empty expanse of moss, but in the mid-nineteenth century increasingly effective attempts were made to reclaim and cultivate the district. In 1863 local landowners, led by

the Squire of Rawcliffe, Wilson F. France, optimistically promoted an 11½-mile railway from Garstang to tiny Knott End, opposite Fleetwood on the other side of the Wyre estuary. The route included the agricultural community of Pilling, from which it derived its porcine nickname. The farmers' main aim was to improve the outlets for their produce by giving easy access to the markets at Preston and in the towns and cities of industrial Lancashire – a straightforward intention, although hyperbole ruled in the extravagant claims the promoters made. The line, they said, would link up with Yorkshire, Humberside and Newcastle upon Tyne, and could become part of a main artery between the east and west coasts. Knott End, where a harbour might be built, would rival and even outgrow Fleetwood. The Garstang and Knott End (as it was then spelt) was incorporated on 30 June 1864 to build 11½ miles of line from Garstang and Catterall station to Knott End. Virtually no earthworks were required in the flat countryside, apart from low embankments at the girder bridge over the Wyre at Garstang and a shallow cutting near the Lancaster Canal.

The Company immediately ran into acute financial difficulties, and after three years the only work accomplished had been the preparation of the trackbed for the first half mile of the route. In December 1867, by which date most of the original capital had been spent, it was decided to abandon plans to build the Pilling-Knott End section. Despite further near-bankruptcy the contractors struggled on, and after a catalogue of delays which augured ill for its future, the line finally opened on 5 December 1870 with a celebration dinner at the Royal Oak Hotel, Garstang. In its publicity material, the operating company described it as 'one of the most interesting and unique railways in the United Kingdom'. Sadly, it was not one of the country's most successful.

For a start, the under-capitalised company had to borrow an engine, the saddle tank *Hebe*. With a solitary locomotive and a mere quartet of carriages, the railway gamely struggled on with no rolling stock in reserve. While the engine was being repaired in March 1872, the line had to close down for two days. Then *Hebe* was seized when the rental payments were not met, and horses had to be used to pull the train. The management had no alternative but to withdraw the passenger service on 11 March 1872 and

goods trains $2\frac{1}{2}$ weeks later. Fifteen months after its opening, the line fell into disuse. An official receiver was appointed and services resumed in 1875 using an 0-4-0 tank, *Union*, bought by debenture holders. The company also purchased an 0-6-0 saddle tank, *Farmer's Friend*, which started work the following year. This followed a bizarre accident in September 1875 when a fierce wind blew two carriages three miles along the line from Pilling.

By 1894, however, the line had paid off its debts. Still, though, the $4\frac{1}{2}$-mile stretch from Pilling to Knott End had to be built. (One local wit said it was appropriate that the line did Not End at Knott End but at Pilling.) An Act of 12 August 1898 authorised the extension but, typically, the project encountered delays. As the Garstang and Knott End Railway Company had no money, a separate company – the Knott End Railway Co. – was formed to build the extension. It was soon in difficulty, but was rescued by a timely geological coincidence – the development of the salt mines at Preesall by the United Alkali Company. The work proceeded with extraordinary slowness – it took ten years to build $4\frac{1}{2}$ miles of line! The two companies decided quite sensibly to amalgamate their operations, and on 1 July 1908 the Knott End Railway Company bought the Garstang and Knot End Company for £50,000 and opened the four-mile 'missing link' to passengers on 29 July. In 1913, 91,918 passengers were carried. Some of the materials that went into the construction of the extension came from Richard Fleetwood's first charity school at Preesall. The school had gradually become more run-down so the contractors demolished it and used the stones for the railway.

In 1912 a branch line, 1½ miles long, was opened from Knott End to serve the United Alkali Company's salt works at Preesall. The branch was the - temporary - saviour of this line. In 1913, the first full year of the salt works, 7,916 tons of salt were carried, but by 1920 this had risen to 53,000 tons, together with 24,000 tons of coal for fuel at the works. In the early 1920s, as a result of this ex-

tra traffic, the line actually made a modest profit. This, however, was soon to disappear as road competition took away its business.

The Pig - an alternative derivation for the sobriquet was the squeal of the loco's shrill whistle over the fields - may not have been profitable but it was undeniably picturesque. Provided the engine did not break down, the passenger had a scenic journey lasting 35 to 40 minutes, from the edge of the River Wyre at Knott End past a series of historic landmarks in the Over Wyre flatlands. There was Parrox Hall, seat of the Elletson family - to this day,

Below:
The end for Knott End. Smiling faces belie the fact that this is the last train from Knott End Station on 13 November 1950. The class 2 2-6-0 No. 46429 was hauling a freight train - it had been 20 years since passengers last travelled on the rural route. The line was to remain open for goods traffic between Pilling and Garstang until 1963, but even now its impact on the landscape can still be seen.

lords of the manor of Preesall – with its remnants of an old racecourse. There was seventeenth-century Hackensall Hall, once moated, Pilling village and Fluke Hall. Despite the level appearance of the landscape and the absence of any significant embankments, there was a gradient of 1:73 at the steepest point between Nateby and Garstang. Intermediate stations were at Garstang Town, Winmarleigh (renamed Nateby on New Year's Day 1902) and, from 1908, Preesall. In addition, there were tiny wayside halts, with signboards but no real platforms, at Cogie Hill and Cockerham Crossing, between Nateby and Pilling. A further halt was opened at Carr Lane, 1½ miles west of Pilling, in 1911. Locals swore that the carriages bore a sign reading, 'Please do not lean out to pick flowers while the train is in motion.' A Mr W. McCormick, a friend of Tom Langley, stationmaster at Knott End Hackensall Crossing, is credited with composing the following ditty, sung to the tune of 'Way Down upon the Swannee River':

Way down upon the Knott End Railway,
Not far away,
They have got a little puffer engine
Which travels a few miles a day.
All the day the driver whistles;
He is out of tune.
If you leave Knott End in September,
You will land at Garstang in June.

Timetables were often suspended for mid-field chats between farmers and engine drivers. As goods trains pulled into the stations, eager farmers fought to claim their produce, sometimes jumping on to still-moving trucks.

The grouping of the railway companies in 1923 saw the line absorbed into the London, Midland and Scottish. Four small tank engines, including the locally named *Blackpool* and her sister *Knott End*, operated the goods service while passengers were carried by an ex-LNWR steam railmotor. The five-strong fleet formed the smallest constituent of the vast LMS empire. The passenger service was to prove short-lived, however, and was withdrawn at the end of March 1930. The Knott End to Pilling section was closed completely on 13 November 1950, after just 42 years, with the rest remaining open for freight between Pilling and Garstang, carrying paper pulp and cattle foods, until 1 August 1963. Garstang Town station stayed open as a coal depot until August 1965.

Garstang's hopes of becoming a railway hub has passed, as had Knott End's of being transformed into a surrogate Fleetwood. Perhaps Garstang's last moments of railway glory came on the nights of 28 August 1940 and 30 October 1941, when King George VI and Queen Elizabeth slept in the royal train there, protected by police and Civil Defence personnel. There was certainly no squealing pig to disturb the royal couple's slumbers.

Chapter Five

HOLIDAY HEYDAY

THE Fylde's railway heyday came between the wars. Despite - or, perhaps, because of - the economic depression and the gathering war clouds on the Continent, holidaymakers poured into Blackpool in astronomical numbers. By the outbreak of World War Two, the resort's two main stations were, during the season, the busiest provincial termini in Britain. The operators faced unique problems, but also incalculable opportunities, as they battled to cope with the hundreds of thousands of day trippers and holidaymakers who thronged the stations every season.

The influx fuelled, and was in turn fuelled by, yet another period of rapid expansion of Blackpool's economy in the 1920s. Before World War One, the resort had decided to increase its allure still further by illuminating the promenade with strings of electrical lights. After the war, there was strong pressure from the Chamber of Trade to revive the attraction as a way of drawing more visitors and extending the holiday season into the autumn. The Illuminations, as they came to be known, were hugely successful, generating a million extra passengers on the promenade trams. The 1926 Illuminations were cut short by the General Strike but the annual extravaganza had already been established as the 'greatest free show on Earth'. Today, the Lights have made Blackpool unique among holiday towns, with a season stretching through until the first week of November, and have helped confirm its position as the nearest thing in the UK to a year-round resort.

As patterns of tourism trade have altered during the early and high season, from May to August, the months of September and October have become ever more vital to the local economy.

Today's tourists crawl through the Illuminations in cars and coaches; in the pre-war period, they travelled by rail to Black-

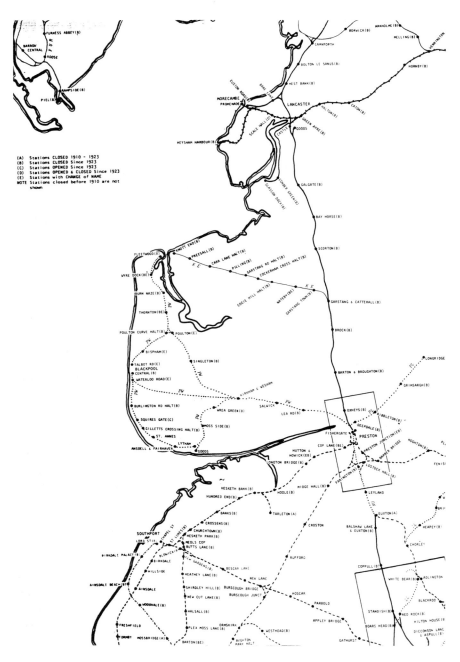

(A) Stations CLOSED 1910 - 1923
(B) Stations CLOSED Since 1923
(C) Stations OPENED Since 1923
(D) Stations OPENED & CLOSED Since 1923
(E) Stations with CHANGE of NAME
NOTE Stations closed before 1910 are not shown

Fylde railways at their peak.

pool and saw the Lights on foot or by tram. Even in the age of Blackpool's present truncated train system, however, the Northern Lights remain a period of frenetic activity for BR.

The inter-war period also saw the decisive development phase

The imposing frontage of Squire's Gate Station soon after its opening in September 1931. BR shared the premises with a bank. The booking office was at road-level, with steps descending from the bridge to the platforms. Located next to an airport and a major holiday centre, the station is still seen by many as ripe for expansion.

of what, after the Tower, is Blackpool's most famous attraction. The Pleasure Beach grew from a ramshackle collection of fairground rides and stalls on the sands at South Shore to become Britain's most visited tourist spot. Founded by William George Bean, and still controlled by his family, the 42-acre amusement park provided the engine for the rapid development of the southern part of the town. It boasted the world's first 15-inch gauge miniature railway from 1905 to 1909, until it was removed because of maintenance difficulties caused by wind-blown sand. However, the park still has an impressive 20-inch gauge miniature railway system, operating in the shadow - literally - of white-knuckle rides like the Revolution, Avalanche and Big Dipper.

The full-sized railway, too, played its part in securing the success of the Pleasure Beach. Apart from the short-lived halt at Burlington Road, however, it was not until 1987 that the amusement park gained its own station. The attractive timber-built structure was opened at a cost of £58,000 with the Thompson family - the descendants of W. G. Bean - providing more than half the cash. Development of the Pleasure Beach in the pre-war period had helped accentuate the process of shifting Blackpool's focal point southwards, a process which - to the chagrin of North Shore business people - continues today. On 14 September 1931, meanwhile, that process was further confirmed when a station was opened on the coastal line at Squire's Gate, on the southern boundary of the resort. This replaced the defunct Stony Hill Station and served the new airport with a long private siding.

Blackpool's relentless growth between the wars placed severe strains on the railway network. The resort, with no fewer than five stations and a halt, became a victim of its own phenomenal success. As early as 1910, 167 specials - both arrivals and departures - were handled by Blackpool's two termini on a single Saturday in August. The town's population was then 65,000, so this volume of traffic was virtually equivalent to evacuating and repopulating the resort in just one day, by excursion trains alone. One memorable excursion for employees of Bass Breweries at Burton-on-Trent had needed no fewer than 17 special trains to transport more than 10,000 workers. By 1919 the L & Y was carrying the heaviest holiday traffic in the country to Blackpool. For certain popular excursion services, large crowds would assemble on the platform, and as the train drew to a halt there would be an undistinguished scramble for seats. The elderly, families with young children and those laden with luggage would be left behind to take their chances on the next train. In an attempt to end the chaos, the railway company introduced a system of 'regulated' trains. For no extra charge, regulated passengers were issued with supplementary tickets bearing the distinguishing number of their train and the date on which they could travel. In this way, supply was matched to demand, and every passenger was guaranteed a seat. The company also had the assurance that all regulated trains would be loaded to capacity. The press inevitably labelled the new system 'rationing of travel', a phrase which stuck, even though it was no more than a form of advance booking to ensure an even flow of passengers during the busiest periods.

Regulation certainly did nothing to deter potential passengers.

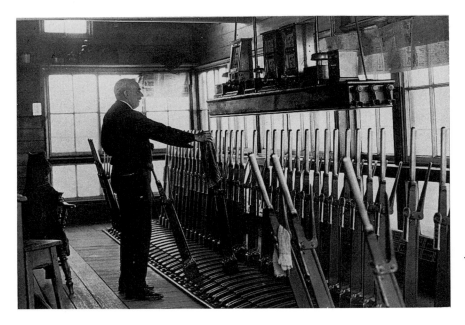

A signal success... this interior shot of Blackpool North No. 1 signal cabin in July 1932 – at the peak of the holiday season – reinforces how much sheer physical strength was needed to shift the heavy manual levers.

An ex-LNWR G2 class 7F 0-8-0 locomotive brings traffic – or, more precisely, a car, a pedestrian and a bicycle – to a halt as it steams through Thornton level crossing.

During the eleven weeks it was in force in the 1919 summer season, almost a million passengers were carried to Blackpool from Manchester and neighbouring towns under the new system. The regulated days were initially Saturday and Monday, but seaside landladies' dislike of split weeks meant that it was the weekend which saw the lion's share of the traffic. Railway operators found themselves facing the task of transporting almost half the season's holiday traffic on Saturdays alone. (In 1920 Fridays and Saturdays became the regulated days.) In just two August weekends, the total number of passengers handled reached 130,000.

Regulation may have controlled the growth but it did not restrain it. By the summer of 1931, it was not unusual for 120 specials, both arrivals and departures, to be dealt with in a single day at each Blackpool terminus. During one week in August 1931, 190,000 tickets were collected –

more than half from passengers who had arrived on the Saturday. The Saturday arrivals were almost equivalent to the town's then resident population of 101,500. The peak period was probably during the dark days of the rise of fascism in mainland Europe. On one Saturday in August 1935, no fewer than 467 trains ran into and out of Blackpool – an astonishing turnover of more than 190,000 passengers. On a typical September Saturday in 1938 – with war just a year away – observers logged 98 down and 52 up train movements, including light engines, between 1.30 p.m. and 6 p.m. The register at Kirkham North junction signal box showed that 90 trains entered Blackpool in three hours – a rate of one every two minutes. The volume of traffic put a huge strain on Blackpool's railway resources. Despite being a pebble's throw from the sea, Blackpool Central Shed often suffered severe water restrictions because

of the flood-tide of trains. Spare tenders were sometimes taken to North Station, where water supplies were better for refilling.

The fact that the Fylde's network could cope with such daunting demands was largely due to the foresight of the men who designed the system. C. B. Byles, the L & Y signal engineer from 1897–1911, was responsible for much of the signalling work which allowed such intensive use of the line. Despite various devices to help them, however, the signalmen in the vast Kirkham North cabin must have been extremely fit to shift the 105 man-

ual levers. It was the same story of metronome-like planning at the stations themselves. The passengers, of course, were largely unaware of this as they were funnelled through the barriers to be met by a chorus of bellowing invitations from the barrow boys offering to cart their luggage to their lodgings. For the arrivals, disembarkation in Blackpool meant seven miles of sands, three piers, four majestic ballrooms, the largest theatre outside the West End - the Opera House - Europe's biggest amusement park and the legendary Golden Mile. For the LMS, into

A classic seaside steam scene … a pillar of smoke rises skywards, in parallel with the Tower in the background, as LMS Jubilee class 4-6-0 no. 5563 'Australia' heads out of Blackpool Central Station. The stretch of track pictured in this evocative worm's-eye-view is now a car and coach park.

which the L & Y was absorbed at 'grouping' in 1923, it meant a major operation to handle and stable the incoming trains – often, in the case of excursions, for only a few hours. To minimise traffic movements, there were plans to build a connecting line between Blackpool North, as Talbot Road was redesignated in 1932, and Blackpool Central, removing the need for reversing trains and complex shunting movements. But the line never materialised. The two stations had no shortage of platform space in which to accommodate the trains, however. Blackpool North had 15 platforms and Central 14, giving a total length of more than 3½ miles. Central signal cabin had 132 levers and Spen Dyke 120, both boxes having been installed in 1901. At the time, Central cabin was the biggest on the L & Y system. Blackpool's excursion traffic between the wars was fostered by Arthur Davies, OBE, who later became the vice-president of the LMS. A former stalwart of the L & Y, he eventually transferred to Euston after grouping but remained faithful to Lancashire and never moved his home from St Annes.

With the excess of excursions, it is easy to forget that the Fylde's rail routes were also used extensively by local passengers. However, one unique development meant that the coast's railway was relieved of many of the locals who might otherwise have used it to travel between Blackpool and North Fylde. This was the Blackpool and Fleetwood Tramway, a precursor of the rapid transit systems that are now in vogue again among public transport planners.

Much has already been written about the tramway, most notably by the prolific Steve Palmer and Brian Turner, so this account must necessarily be brief. After the opening of the original Blackpool conduit system in 1885, the pioneering tramway was steadily extended south as far as Squire's Gate. In 1898 the Blackpool and Fleetwood Tramroad Company opened a standard-gauge system on sleeper track along the clifftops between the two resorts. The southern terminus was at Talbot Road Station. There were eight 'stations' along the tramway, which survive today. The line was bought by Blackpool Corporation on New Year's Eve 1919, when, 20 years after the conversion of the promenade line from conduit to overhead wires, the two were joined at Gynn Square. The tramway was connected to the Lytham St Annes system at Starr Gate, and there was a proposal to link it to Southport's via a transporter bridge across the Ribble. There was even a scheme to link Gynn Square to Garstang and the west-coast main line, but it failed to reach fruition.

However, there were already connections between the tram system and the railway. In 1904 a single-track loop line was laid from the railway sidings at Rigby Road into the tram depot. The L & Y and LNWR had also sought powers in 1918 to build a branch line to Cleveleys but, instead, reached an agreement under which the tramway was connected with the railway at Fleetwood. A steeple cab electric loco hauled trains of wagons from the connecting line with the LMS tracks behind Copse Road depot at Fleetwood to the Thornton Gate mineral sidings in Cleveleys. The wagons were then shunted on to a spur line and unloaded into bunkers at the track side, where several coal merchants had their offices. After a series of disputes between Blackpool Corporation and the merchants, the last mineral train ran on 30 April 1949. The 10-ton tram engine is now preserved at the National Tramway Museum.

In Blackpool, meanwhile, the network had been extended along a series of suburban routes, including Marton and Layton. The rise of the motor car saw the abandonment of all the town's street tramways in the 1960s, but the coast line remains Britain's last surviving traditional electric tramway of any note, bolstered by the introduction of new rolling stock, including one-man operated vehicles, and by track renewal schemes.

But Blackpool was not just an important terminal for tourist excursions: it was also a leading destination for scheduled express services from London and other key conurbations. One of its prides in the immediate pre-war period was the Blackpool and Fylde Coast Express, which left Euston at 5.10 p.m. every weekday and arrived at Central at 9.53 p.m. The morning train left Central at 8.25 a.m. and reached London four hours and 25 minutes later, hauled by Patriot class 4-6-0 No. 5524 *Blackpool*. Up the coast, however, the crack Fleetwood–Belfast boat train, the Ulster Express, was switched to Heysham in 1928. By the mid-1930s, though, the clouds of conflict were descending and troops were to replace tourists as the railway's customers. It was a challenge to which the Fylde's network readily responded.

Chapter Six

TRAINS AND TRAGEDY

INEVITABLY, on such a busy network, all did not run entirely smoothly for the Fylde's railway operators. The coast has witnessed three major railway accidents causing serious loss of life. Yet, though each fatality was a personal tragedy, the toll of 23 deaths from the three disasters is remarkably small considering the 150-year history of the network. It is certainly only a fraction of the number of deaths caused on the Fylde's roads.

Poulton, 1893

The trippers felt content with life as their train began to steam out of Talbot Road Station. The three-carriage holiday special was taking the visitors home - most of them to Wigan - after a summer day out in Blackpool. A few minutes later, however, as the train rounded a sharp curve at Poulton Station, their laughter turned to terror as the locomotive lurched from the rails. The engine ploughed up the ground, reeling to the left, and fell helplessly on to its side, steam still gushing from its valves. The driver, Cornelius Ridgway, of Stockport, lay dead. His fireman, William Lowe, also from Stockport, was thrown clear.

It was soon after 11 p.m. on Saturday, 1 July 1893. Rescuers rushing to the scene found a vista of devastation. The tender lay upside-down. A first-class carriage had been hurled upwards, with one end resting seven feet up on a coal wagon. The other two coaches had broken from their bogies, and splintered wood and shattered glass lay everywhere. Some of the passengers had managed to scramble from the wreckage; others had to be lifted out. The final toll was three dead, including a 14-year-old chorister on a church choir picnic, and 36 injured. Two Poulton doctors were soon on the scene, joined later by colleagues from across the Fylde. It was the coast's first major rail crash, but it could have been even worse if an intending passenger at Poulton had not lost his ticket. The hold-up at the ticket barrier delayed the departure of the last train for Blackpool - which would have been rounding the curve at the same time as the oncoming train left the rails.

The accident confirmed the worst fears of many Poulton residents who had long warned of the potential dangers caused by such a sharp curve. There was even a question in Parliament. On 1 September - exactly two months after the tragedy - it was announced that a Board of Trade inquiry had found the accident had resulted mainly from high speed on the curve. The report noted with satisfaction that the railway companies intended to build a new station at Poulton and remove the tragically tight curve (see Chapter Three).

Lytham, 1924

No-one on board the 4.40 p.m. 'businessmen's express' from Liverpool to Blackpool Central could have suspected what lay ahead as it approached a curve 1½ miles before Lytham. The four-coach train was filled with the chatter of clerks and mill girls letting off steam as they returned from their offices and factories after another uneventful Monday - 3 November 1924. A passenger glanced at his watch. Soon the train would be pulling into Lytham Station, where it was due at 5.46 p.m. It never arrived. Within seconds, the driver and 12 passengers lay dead or dying, and 35 people were injured, in the Fylde's worst rail disaster. In a few moments of terror, the engine left the rails and ploughed headlong into a signal box, reducing it to matchwood. The coaches careered in the wake of the locomotive, the first two toppling over, the last bursting into flames. But, like the Poulton crash of 1893, it could have been worse: a second tragedy was only averted by alert passengers rushing down the line to warn an oncoming train.

It had seemed just like any other Monday afternoon when the train left Liverpool Exchange an hour earlier. The service was popular with businessmen and clerical staff returning home to the Fylde from offices in the city. At Kirkham, weavers from the local mill joined the train. As it started to negotiate the slight curve at Warton Crossing near Eastham, however, the train began to rock and then left the track, flinging passengers crazily across the coaches. The 4-4-0 loco ended up hundreds of yards along the line, although, amazingly, the signalman from the demolished box survived after being flung into a field. The *Blackpool Gazette and Herald* reported:

'For a few moments after the first rending, tearing crash, which none who heard it will forget, there was a deadly silence. It was only momentary. The last coach burst into flames, and simultaneously the cries of the injured broke the still air.

'The light of the flames lit up a tragic scene. The twisted, torn train lay in a confused tangle. The track was pulled up as if it had been a plaything. Already passengers, injured and uninjured, were making their escape through the windows. Others, pinned down, were crying for help.'

Sixty years after the crash, survivor Arthur Ogden told the *Evening Gazette* of his own, amazing escape. The 17-year-old commuter normally travelled in the leading coach but, by a quirk of fate that probably saved his life, got into the second carriage for the fateful trip. He recalled:

'I felt a bumping and shuddering, and I threw myself down on the floor, possibly escaping some damage as a result. But eventu-

ally the carriage turned over, slid and crashed.'

After a strenuous effort, he and his friends managed to force open a window and begin their escape from the wreckage.

'The next thing I remember – I must have been temporarily knocked out – was my friend pulling me up. We helped each other climb the luggage rack, which was then vertical. Then we did what we could to help the other passengers.'

Doctors from Blackpool, Lytham St Annes and Preston were rushed to the accident, and Lytham 'steam fire brigade' got to work on the burning coach. Among the casualties was Commander C. H. Greame, RNR, the captain of the White Star liner *Bardic.* He spoke cheerfully to his rescuers despite terrible leg injuries from which he later died. Three of a group of six mill girls were killed within 15 minutes of boarding the train at Kirkham and Wesham.

And the cause of the crash? It was due, a Ministry of Transport inquiry concluded, to failure of an engine tyre.

Weeton, 1961

The carriages pointing bizarrely skywards formed a macabre memorial to the seven who died in one of the Fylde coast's most appalling civil disasters. The death toll was not as great as the Lytham crash of 1924, but 116 people were injured at

Weeton in 1961 – and the photographs of the gruesome aftermath remain etched on the minds of all who have seen them.

It was 10.25 a.m. on a summer Sunday as the six-car diesel multiple unit sped through the Fylde fields carrying 350 trippers bound for Fleetwood and the Isle of Man ferry. They had left Colne at 8.50 p.m. on that ill-fated day, 16 July, in high spirits. But a tragic misunderstanding between signalmen at Singleton and Weeton saw the trip end in disaster on Singleton Bank. The DMU ploughed into the back of a stationary ballast train, leap-frogging the wagons and jack-knifing. Six people in the packed passenger train were killed, and a seventh died of his injuries three days later.

A public inquiry put the blame on a signalman, while criticising several other railmen, and inquest verdicts of misadventure were returned on the dead. The official accident report found that the rules governing the bal-lasting operation had been constantly broken. With one line closed, the job of signalling trains along the remaining track was being done on a wing and a prayer rather than by the book. An inexperienced signalman gave a 'line clear' signal for the Fleetwood bound unit without receiving a cancelling signal for the ballast train.

The Colne–Fleetwood train passed Weeton signal box at 60 mph, trying to make up for lost time. As the ballast train came into view, the DMU driver, Thomas Shaw, aged 61, bravely stayed at the controls and slammed on his brakes in a vain attempt to avert a collision. A lesser man might have set the brakes and then run back down

Below:
Carriages are skewed crazily skyward after the 8.50am from Colne ploughs in the rear of a stationary ballast train on Singleton Bank, killing seven and injuring 116, in July 1961. The accident that saw the Fleetwood-bound DMU leap-frog the wagons was the result of a tragic misunderstanding between signal men. It is said the earth around the embankment still bears the scars of the crash.

the corridor to escape the full impact. Driver Shaw was killed instantly as the DMU ran into the 575-ton ballast train, whose guard had just enough time to leap clear before his van was crushed to pieces. Forty men on the ballast train jumped down the embankment, fortunately on the other side from the plummeting diesel unit. Within minutes, a huge rescue operation was set in motion, and ambulances from all over the Fylde – including a vehicle from nearby RAF Weeton – converged on the scene.

Less than 24 hours later, a BR inquiry started in Preston and sat day and night to hear 23 witnesses and compile a report for the Ministry of Transport. The following week, a two-day public inquiry was held in Manchester. The inquest jury's eventual misadventure verdicts were based on 'the misunderstanding of and the non-compliance with the signalling regulations and rules as laid down by British Railways'.

Almost 30 years after the tragedy, new light was shed on the disaster by a retired railwayman who, but for a twist of fate, would have been travelling on the doomed train. The Blackpool-based railman was the rostered guard for the boat train but was asked to exchange shifts as another guard did not know the 'road' to Euston. The Blackpool guard knew all the arrangements for the ballast train and he confirmed the accident had been due to a series of misunderstandings. Taken alone, they might just have caused a nuisance; together, they made up a lethal combination. The guard wrote:

'The signals at Weeton Box were misunderstood by the train crew as to the ballast train being there. The intention was to let the diesel pass the signal box, stop, and reverse to the (wrong road) up line and proceed to Poulton No. 1.

'But, first, there was a change of guards, second, the signals should have been on until the train had stopped, then proceeded slowly past the signal until the rear cleared the crossover, and reversed.

'I feel that a series of minor mistakes that dreadful Sunday led to the disaster.'

To this day, regular travellers on the line say they can still detect the scars left by the wrecked coaches on the embankment. As one old countryman reflected: 'it's as if the earth was weeping for its dead.'

Yet the ultimate indomitability of the human spirit was demonstrated by the fact that many passengers were able to continue their journey to Douglas later that day – and on Monday services were back to normal.

Chapter Seven

DECADES OF DECLINE

THE remarkable irony of the railway in wartime was that a system built to handle pleasure seekers could so easily be adapted to the needs of people dealing in the deadly serious business of warfare. The rail infrastructure was of pivotal importance in wartime strategy on the home front. With evacuees, civil servants, servicemen and trippers - defying the prevailing gloom - streaming to the Fylde coast, Blackpool's rail system remained among the most heavily used in the country.

Even before the outbreak of war, there was a mood of almost unrealistic confidence in the resort. The 1939 season saw the completion of a series of major developments, including the Odeon Cinema, the new Opera House, the now demolished Derby Pool, the Pleasure Beach Casino building - Joseph Emberton's striking, circular Art Deco masterpiece - and the Talbot Road bus station. The number of visitors to Blackpool had fallen by 10 per cent in 1938 as the European crisis deepened but 1939 was a boom season as trippers enjoyed a final fling before the inevitable conflict. The number of rail passengers at Easter and Whitsun was 20 per cent higher than the previous record two years earlier. Even during the Phoney War, the holidaymakers continued to come, encouraged by government exhortations to families to take their normal holidays as a morale booster. By this time, though, the railways had taken on a more sombre role.

Within an hour of Neville Chamberlain's ultimatum to Hitler expiring on 3 September 1939, the first trains packed with evacuee children were pulling into Central Station. Volunteers and nurses were at the barriers to welcome the arrivals from industrial Lancashire, some weeping, all with their gas mask cases. More than 37,000 arrived in the first three days. Nationally, an incredible 1.5 million people were evacuated, mostly by rail.

*Central swan song…
trippers from Oldham,
beaming expectantly, pour
out of a special train at
Blackpool Central in 1963.
Barely a year after this
picture was taken, Central
was closed and sold to the
council for redevelopment –
to the astonishment of
Blackpool's railway
community. But the outlines
of the platforms where these
visitors stood are still visible
beneath the car park which,
inevitably, has taken the
place of the station.*

With its vast reserves of hotel accommodation, Blackpool was also a natural location for civil service complexes when they were moved out of London and the Home Counties. A total of 45 hotels were requisitioned by ministries. But it was forces personnel, particularly the RAF, who were to form the biggest clientage for the Fylde's railways during the war. More than ¾ million RAF recruits did their basic training in Blackpool. They were joined by tens of thousands of airmen stationed at RAF Weeton and Kirkham, while the USAAF had a larger base at Warton aerodrome. It all led to extraordinary scenes on August Bank Holiday 1940 when so many people poured into the resort that it was impossible to find accommodation for them all and many had to sleep rough.

Despite Blackpool's strategic importance, it escaped comparatively lightly from Luftwaffe bombing raids. The only serious bombing incident was in 1940 when a German aircraft, apparently trying to unload its bombs on North Station, missed the target and hit nearby Seed Street, killing eight people. But Blackpool's worst wartime air disaster involved no enemy aircraft. At about 3.15 p.m. on 27 August 1941, a Boulton Paul Defiant aircraft clipped the rear of a Blackburn Botha, part of which then plunged on to Central Station. The rest of the plane dropped into the sea, killing its two RAF pilot officers. A civilian mechanic crashed with the front section of the Botha into the station, where it killed thirteen other people. The Defiant crashed onto a house in Read's Avenue, with its young New Zealand pilot. His colleague, also a New Zealander, was discovered in Regent Road, an unopened parachute on his body. An RAF court of inquiry attached no blame to the pilot of either aircraft. In all, the death toll was eighteen, but it could have been much worse: only moments before the crash, a packed train had left the station.

Despite the resort's relatively lenient treatment by the Luftwaffe, the railways were taking no chances. The Rigby Road motive powered depot was kept in near darkness so as not to attract the attentions of enemy aircraft. The lack of light did not prevent staff working away doggedly maintaining the 50 locomotives based at the two Blackpool sheds.

Victory in Europe and the Far East brought a new mood of optimism to the country after six years of war and hardship. Clement Attlee's Labour Government was elected on a pledge to build a new era for Britain, both economically and socially. At a more parochial level, this upbeat mood was reflected by visitors beginning to pour back into Blackpool. A record 102,889 arrived by rail on one summer Saturday in 1945. Even the austerity years of the immediate post-war period could not deter them. From the early 1950s, however, there was a scent of decline in the air.

The roads to Blackpool had been crowded with traffic since car ownership began to grow significantly in the 1930s. After the abolition of petrol rationing in 1950, motorists headed for the Fylde in ever increasing numbers, and the railway's share of the traffic began to dwindle. The internal combustion engine was here to stay. Nationally, Lancashire was a leader in motorway development: ironically, it was at Preston - rail gateway to the Fylde - that Britain's first motorway was built. Ironically, too, it was the brainchild of the county surveyor, Sir James Drake - formerly Blackpool's borough engineer and surveyor. The Preston bypass, now part of the M6, was opened in December 1958. Even so, the railways in the 1950s remained busy up to the closing years of the decade. There were few clues to the scale of the contraction that was to come. A survey during the first day of the

A Tower-top view of Blackpool Central shortly before its closure in 1964. The excursion platforms are on the left, next to Central Drive. All that now remains is the toilet block, the pennies from which were said to have paid for the station's rates bill.

1959 Illuminations, for instance, recorded 152 down and 112 up train movements between 8 a.m. and 8 p.m. to and from Blackpool. Movements through Kirkham between 1.30 p.m. and 6 p.m. totalled 47 down and 25 up – about half the figures for 1938 given in Chapter Five. That evening, there were 37 return excursion trains in 3½ hours - roughly one departure every five minutes.

But the bigger they are, the harder - and more painfully - they fall. The Blackpool rail network had enjoyed more than a century of prosperity, so when the fall came, it was spectacular. Göring had failed to bomb the railway into submission, but the rise of the motor car, the Beeching Report, and local and national government indifference - bordering on antipathy - achieved the same result by stealth. The railway had built

Blackpool, but the town council, once it had reaped the network's benefits, was only too anxious to discard it. By the mid 1950s, the railway was becoming an embarrassment, occupying prime town-centre sites that could more usefully be taken up by car parks and bingo halls.

It had not always been so. The expansion of the railway in its early years had been a classic example of a partnership between private and public enterprise. The burghers of Blackpool, and the panjandrums of the railway companies co-operated in an alliance of typically Victorian pragmatism - of mutual self- interest. What went wrong? Why did this admittedly mercenary but nonetheless effective collaboration turn into fractious distrust over the next century?

At first, it seems, it was the rail-

Before and after views of the maze of marshalling yards between Blackpool Central and South Stations. The first, taken from the air by former Evening Gazette photographic manager Raymond Hoyle, shows the main line and sidings in 1964, with the football ground and rugby league stadium to the right of the engine sheds. The second, nine years later, shows the same area, stripped starkly of rail tracks and ready for the asphalt.

No expense was spared when the Queen and the Duke of Edinburgh visited Blackpool in the royal train to attend a special performance in their honour at the Opera House. A team of workmen were employed to re-lay and level the sidings where the train was to stay overnight in April 1955. Double-headed class 5 4-6-0s Nos. 45020 and 45045 hauled the royal carriages from the sidings, which were on the original route to Fleetwood. Poulton Station can be seen in the background under the bridge, leading to the realigned Fleetwood curve.

way's fault. During the rail boom of the 1870s, the L & Y acquired a reputation for cavalier treatment of its passengers. The company's third-class carriages were unheated, unlit and had no upholstery. Blackpool Council received increasing numbers of complaints about the company's fares – as high, it was said, as its services were slow. The L & Y was the senior partner (with the LNWR) in running the Fylde's network, but it viewed the coast as just an outpost of its giant empire. In 1884 a delegation from Blackpool approached the railway companies to press for new lines and better services. The delegation was worried that passengers were beginning to shun Blackpool and instead head for better connected rivals like Morecambe. The companies, however, said they had enough to do merely coping with existing business. So the corporation, in typically expansive mood, resolved that it would build a new railway itself. The line would bypass the bottleneck of Preston, which handled up to 500 trains a day, by skirting the town to the south and passing through Lytham St Annes to a new station in the centre of Blackpool, next to the Winter Gardens. Supported by the town hall and the large entertainment operators, a company was formed to build the line with the help of the Great Central Railway, which would construct another route to connect the Blackpool line to the GCR system in south Lancashire.

The land was acquired and the Blackpool Railway Bill was promoted in the House of Commons in 1884. The minutes of the Bill hint at dissatisfaction felt over

Right: Almost the last train of its line ... Black 5 4-6-0 No. 44950 steams into Blackpool South in May 1968, the final spring of steam.

Below: A spectacular aerial shot of the sweeping junction at Blackpool South Station in 1964. Curving away to the right is the former New Line through Marton, now the Yeadon Way motor way link road. Arching to the left is the coast line to Lytham St Annes and Kirkham. Of this striking configuration of track, only a single line remains, linking the former platform one at Blackpool South to stations on the South Fylde line.

A rush of steam provides an atmosphere send-off for former Fleetwood-based Black 5 4-6-0 No. 45212 as it stands at Blackpool South with a train from Preston. Enthusiasts line the platform in August 1968 on the last weekend of regular steam working on British Railways. From then, only the throb of diesels and the hum of electrics would be heard on BR.

the standards of service provided by the Blackpool railway operators. 'There is no doubt', say the minutes, 'that if Blackpool had increased, as it has in a very marvellous manner in the last 30 years, it has not so increased in consequence of railway facilities but rather in spite of the railway accommodation which has been afforded to it'. However, construction of the railway was constantly delayed until, in the 1890s, it faded quietly from the agenda. But it did have the result of shaking the L & Y out of its complacency and forcing it to embark on the infrastructure improvements it made towards the end of the century.

Rail-council relations continued on a relatively even keel during the first part of the twentieth century, but the early quarrels had embittered the town hall's decision makers. As early as the mid 1930s, council planners had come to realise the development potential if the corporation could get its hands on the lucrative Central Station site. The land, on the threshold of the Golden Mile, had become a thorn in the side of the council's embryonic masterplan for developing the heart of the resort. The railway itself was not an entirely reluctant partner in all this. A hugely ambitious scheme was to have started in November 1940, with the LMS and the corporation sharing the £2 million cost of redeveloping the entire Central Station site. The station was to have been replaced by a much bigger building in Chapel Street, leaving the land to the north to be redeveloped with car-parks, a municipal complex and entertainment centres. War put paid to that scheme, but the reprieve for the old station building was to last less than a quarter of a century. Even during the war, however, the council was quietly pursuing its goal of dislodging the railway from its town-centre enclaves.

An illuminating insight into the council's enthusiasm for ridding the centre of the resort of its railway is provided by a report to councillors in April 1944 by James Drake, before he went on to pioneer motorway development as Lancashire's county surveyor, and was awarded a knighthood.

In his report, he called for the setting back of Central Station as far as Bloomfield Road, releasing almost 130 acres of land for redevelopment. He lamented the piecemeal way in which that part of Blackpool had been allowed to develop into a 'characterless mass', with railways, tram sheds, houses, shops, factories and gas works all jostling together with no coherent plan. It was, he said, that nightmare of the Victorian era: development which had been controlled and regulated by the building by-laws only. Joining the two areas of corporation land split by the railway would increase their value tenfold. The panacea for all this reckless individualism was, of course, planning. Sir James was a brilliant and imaginative engineer, but he and his elected colleagues exhibited all the boundless self-confidence and rectitude of those for whom 'planning' was the ultimate lode-star. He wrote:

'[The area] must be put to its best economic efficiency for the community and well-being of the individual. It may mean the

The buffet sign on the old Blackpool North Station must have looked inviting to the man wheeling a pram along Dickson Road on a thoroughly wet and windswept morning in Blackpool. This 1898 structure was demolished to make way for a supermarket, with a new terminus opening on the site of the former excursion platforms in 1974. The tram service between Fleetwood and North Station, via the Gynn and Dickson Road, closed in 1963.

subordination to the public good of the personal interests and wishes of the various owners, but the individuality of the town must be retained and this can only be done by bold planning...'

Noble sentiments, but almost 50 years on, Sir James' profession has been forced to restrict itself to more modest aims; its philosophy is far less sanguine. It took another 20 years for the corporation finally to dislodge Central Station, but the Drake dream of a comprehensive redevelopment of the railway land still remains far from reality.

The piquancy of rail's final surrender in Blackpool was that it was achieved with little effort on the council's part. In 1963 a report, The Reshaping of British Railways, proposed ripping up a third of the network and scrapping uneconomic excursion train fleets. Its author, Dr Richard Beeching, a brilliant former ICI physicist, concluded that Blackpool needed only one railway terminal, and that North Station should go. The council was horrified. If any station should go, said the town hall, it should be Central. Representations were made in high places, and they proved effective. Astonishingly, it was decided that Central rather than North should be axed. The decision still provokes bewilderment almost 30 years later. Books still regularly claim that Central Station was a victim of the Beeching axe, when in fact it was the victim of skilful politicking. Central Station, in the shadow of the Tower, was the gateway to the Golden Mile. It was ideally placed

to maximise railway – and resort – revenue, unlike the less accessible North Station. Beleaguered British Railways could be forgiven for agreeing to sell the more valuable of the two sites. Yet, in the event, BR received less than £1 million for the prime 24-acre plot. One leading councillor's description of the deal as a bargain must rank as the understatement of the decade.

Conflicting quotations highlight the difference between the official and the rail lobby views of the shutdown. In July 1964 Harry Porter, Blackpool's director of attractions and publicity, said 'This decision will now crystallise the whole position of the development of this important area of Blackpool. I think it will ultimately prove to be to the advantage of Blackpool.'

Twenty-five years later, however, Malcolm Richardson, vice chairman of the South Fylde Line Users' Association, claimed:

'Closure of Central Station was the most momentous mistake the town ever made. They said it would be the answer to all Blackpool's problems but just look at the traffic congestion last week [the final week of the 1989 Illuminations].'

Perhaps the most poignant comment came from a railwayman with 44 years' service, who described the decision as a cardinal error of judgement. He added:

'I would say responsibility must be shared between BR management and Blackpool Corporation, who were avid to get the site. When they shut Blackpool

Central, they cut the heart out of Blackpool.'

Indeed, many Fylde folk date Blackpool's decline from the sale of the Central site.

Blackpool Council set enthusiastically about its task of developing the Central area. The demolition operation included the removal of 2,310 tons of rail and 39,000 sleepers. At first, the station building remained intact, occupied by a bingo hall, but now only the toilet block remains. The platforms have been filled in and are the site of - predictably - a car park. The rest of the sprawling acreage is taken up by law courts, a high rise police station, a multi-storey car park and the Coral Island amusement complex. The track bed and sidings between the Central site and South Station have been transformed into one of Europe's biggest car and coach park, connected to the M55 by the £4.6 million Yeadon Way link road. Incongruously, this runs along the embankments that once carried the New Line into the resort. The road lobby was at last triumphant.

But there was little magnanimity in victory: the council consistently showed a negative attitude, verging on hostility, toward the railways on which the town's prosperity was founded. Even a proposal for a restored single track line from South Station to Chapel Street, on the extreme western edge of the swathes of tarmac, was received with little enthusiasm. At the same time, though, council leaders were demanding meetings (shades of

1884) to protest to BR about standards of services. It seemed, too, that the council's appetite for acquiring railway land had not been completely satisfied. There were rumours that the town hall wanted to annexe the railway line between South Station and the Pleasure Beach, making Burlington Road the terminus and using the new land as an extension to the Yeadon Way car park. Another rumour had it that the Pleasure Beach itself wanted to buy the land to add to its own, constricted car parking.

But it also has to be said that BR has not been without complicity in all this, forced to sell off land in a depressed market to help balance its books. So far, none of the more Machiavellian speculation has become reality. However, the council did pay £140,000 for 3.5 acres of land next to the BR Staff Association Club in Hampton Road, South Shore. The town hall pledged the land would stay as playing fields in the short term, but few people doubted the triangular site - next to Yeadon Way - would end up as yet another vehicle park. One of the corporations's few gestures of largesse towards the railway came when it part-funded the new Pleasure Beach Station, which opened in April 1987 at cost of £58,000. Yet Blackpool was the junior partner, providing £2,000, compared with the Pleasure Beach's £31,000, BR (£15,000) and Lancashire County Council (£10,000). Transport campaigners are hoping the new Labour administration - which in May 1991 took control for the first time in the town's history -

Wealthy American Rogers Whitaker brings a transatlantic greeting to class A4 Pacific 4-6-2 No. 60022 'Mallard'. Mr Whitaker had flown 3,500 miles just to travel on this famous locomotive, which is pictured at Blackpool North in 1961.

Crowds mill around the legendary Flying Scotsman as it arrives at Blackpool North on 8 October 1966, decorated with the special nameplate, 'Blackpool Belle'. The ex-LNER A3 Pacific attracted the interest of both rail buffs and the simply curious, as the photograph demonstrates.

will demonstrate a more pro-rail attitude.

Apart from peak Illuminations weekends, large tracts of the new car parks remain empty. Contrast that with a single, simple statistic: even on Central's final day, there were no fewer than 55 departures from that station alone. Rail was in decline, but it remained the most effective means of moving large numbers of people with the minimum of environmental disturbance. The last train steamed out of Central Station at the end of the 1964 Illuminations, on 1 November. At the same time, the entire track north of South Station was abandoned and the south shed, once the base for dozens of locomotives, closed. The site also included shops, houses and a large railwaymen's hostel. On the same day, the direct train service between Fleetwood and Blackpool was withdrawn, its functions having long been duplicated by the trams. Blackpool North Shed, which closed on 10 February 1964, had to be brought back into use. The pattern which eventually emerged was for east Lancashire trains to use Blackpool

Fleetwood was where it all began, and where it all ended. Britannia Pacific class 4-6-2 No. 70013 'Oliver Cromwell' prepares to leave the port's Wyre Dock Station, watched by steam stalwarts, on 20 April 1968 – four months before the end of steam on BR.

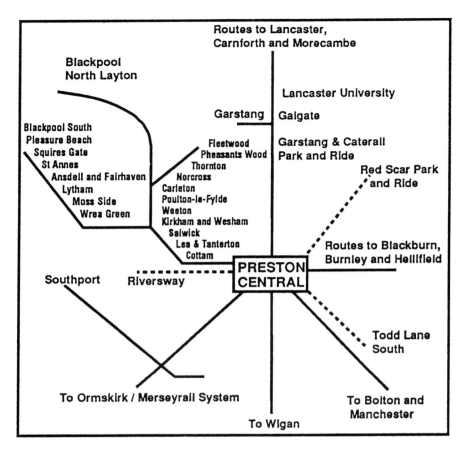

Routes to Lancaster,
Carnforth and Morecambe

Blackpool
North Layton

Lancaster University

Garstang Galgate

Blackpool South
Pleasure Beach   Fleetwood
Squires Gate   Pheasants Wood   Garstang & Caterall
St Annes   Thornton   Park and Ride
Ansdell and Fairhaven   Norcross
Lytham   Carleton   Red Scar Park
Moss Side   Poulton-le-Fylde   and Ride
Wrea Green   Weeton
Kirkham and Wesham
Salwick
Lea & Tanterton   Routes to Blackburn,
Cottam   Burnley and Hellifield

Southport   Riversway   PRESTON
CENTRAL

Todd Lane
South

To Ormskirk / Merseyrail System   To Bolton and
Manchester

To Wigan

Party lines... this is the Lancashire Liberal Democrat blueprint for a county light rapid transit 'metro' system. It would include new stations at Fleetwood, Pheasants' Wood, Thornton, Norcross, Carleton, Weeton, Lea, Wrea Green and Garstang. But some rail campaigners fear the scheme could jeopardise existing 'heavy rail' links in the Fylde.

North, with Manchester and London services using South, which was now the terminus for the coast line. This pattern would be reversed just six years later.

Cuts continued to come. In autumn 1965 the Marton line was closed, although it was used sporadically for a few months afterwards. In May 1970 BR designated North Station the principal terminus for the resort and the London and Manchester services were switched from Blackpool South. The wheel had turned full circle. The decision to concentrate services on North Station left Blackpool South with just a shuttle service to Kirkham, apart from a handful of commuter trains to Manchester. There was constant speculation that South would shut completely, and in January 1971 a 1,060-name petition calling for its retention was sent to the divisional manager of BR's London Midland Region by Blackpool South MP Sir Peter Blaker. BR justified its decision to downgrade South Station by pointing to the difficulty of having to man two stations, with duplication of staff and services. As North was the larger of the two – with sixteen platforms against South's four - and was more centrally situated, it seemed the more logical location for principal services. However, North Station did not entirely escape the all-pervasive axe. Since January 1974, the terminus has occupied the former excursion platforms, the original building having been demolished to make way for a supermarket . . . and a town centre bypass.

Up the coast at Fleetwood, meanwhile, the diary of decline went on. The lsle of Man steamers continued to use the great wooden landing stage beside Fleetwood Station each summer until its was condemned in 1961. Despite the withdrawal of the through service between Fleetwood and Blackpool in 1964 (only two passengers made the last journey), trains continued to run into the imposing quayside terminus at Fleetwood until 1966. On 18 April a rebuilt Wyre Dock Station became the terminus, and the track and landing stage north of Wyre Dock level crossing were dismantled. Sceptics claim the decision to switch the station to the inconveniently sited Wyre Dock was merely a tactic to discourage usage and, ultimately, to close the line on revenue grounds. (Conspiracy theorists detect a similar, though unsuccessful, strategy in the controversy over the Settle-Carlisle line). The Queen's Terrace station at Fleetwood was demolished in 1969. Another casualty of the railway retreat had been the port's once-bustling locomo-

tive depot, where more than 50 passenger, freight and shunting engines were serviced. The passenger service to Poulton was finally withdrawn in 1970 - 130 years after Sir Peter Hesketh Fleetwood's first train to his eponymous port - and now only infrequent tanker trains operate to ICI's Hillhouse chemicals plant at Burn Naze. The superfluous spur to Fleetwood power station closed in 1981, but an enthusiastic preservation group has relaid a short length. The Fleetwood Locomotive Centre, founded in 1981, has an impressive roster of engines ranging from an Avonside Saddleback, salvaged from a children's playground, to the 1943 Stanier Black 5 No 45491 and the magnificent ex-GWR loco *Wootton Hall*.

Lesser incisions took place throughout the 1970s and early 1980s. The 22 miles of marshalling yard between Blackpool South and the former Central Station site were torn up, and the line between Blackpool South and Kirkham singled. It now resembles a remote rural branch rather than the vibrant rail artery it once was. Sunday services were withdrawn in summer 1981. Station buildings were demolished and platforms demanned; a line that once reverberated to expresses every few minutes was left with an hourly service operated by bus-like multiple units. Was it the end of the line for the Fylde's once-flourishing railway system?

Chapter Eight

THE CENTRAL QUESTION

THE final act in the 101-year saga of Blackpool Central Station was played out in an atmosphere of almost Victorian melodrama. Mist swirled across the station – at times visibility was down to twenty yards – and onlookers shivered in the November chill. As the curtain finally fell, however, melodrama gave way to bathos: the last train into the station was late and there was only a smattering of passengers on board. A station which for more than a century had welcomed millions to the threshold of the Golden Mile had been reduced to a near deserted hulk.

It was shortly before midnight on Sunday, 1 November – the last day of the 1964 Illuminations – that the lights went out permanently at Blackpool Central. As the final train rolled into the terminus, an *Evening Gazette* reporter observed: 'Gloomy station staff went about their routine work for the last time as a thick fog drifted over the station, making the whole place cold, damp and rather eerie.'

Earlier, right on time, the last train to leave Central slipped out of platform three at 9.55 p.m. *en route* for London Euston, waved off by its guard, Joseph Cunningham, of North Shore. It was watched by a large crowd of enthusiasts with cameras, sentimentalists and the simply curious. The last sound was the setting-off of three detonators which had been placed on the line in an unofficial commemoration of that poignantly historic event.

The last train to arrive, a diesel from Manchester Victoria, had been due in at 10.58 p.m. but it was past 11.30 p.m. when the driver, Tom Eastham, of Jamieson Street, Blackpool, sounded the hooter as it approached the station. After the train had pulled

First, a fleeting glimpse of the Tower across the flatness of the Fylde's fields. Then, pulling into Blackpool Central, virtually at the foot of the famous landmark. These are the twin memories of generations of Blackpool rail travellers. This post-war picture shows the typical bustle around Blackpool Central, a pebble's throw from the beach.

into the fog-shrouded platforms, he was greeted with a kiss from his wife and a bottle of beer from his son.

'It's a very sad day for me', said 62-year-old Mr Eastham, who was accompanied by his guard, Wilfred Preston, of Bispham.

Fastened to the station barrier, the back cover of a railway time-table had been used to make an improvised notice. After announcing that the axe would fall, it read 'Amen. The end of the road is nigh'.

The station was locked up for the last time by the stationmaster, J. W. Atkinson, flanked by one of his predecessors, Victor Hazeld-

ene. 'It's a shame', Mr Hazeldene reflected. 'It is a very bad mistake closing this station'.

Meanwhile, three hours earlier, a service that had been running for 65 years also ended when the 8.56 p.m. train pulled out of Fleetwood for Blackpool North, with its pair of passengers on board. It was the final through train between the two seaside towns. The service, said a railway spokesman, had been mainly used by ICI workers. Appropriately, the train was manned by two Fleetwood railwaymen – driver Jack Fletcher and guard Thomas Yates.

Back at Blackpool Central,

within hours of the final train pulling out, the gutting of the station began in earnest. Post Office engineers moved in to take out the telephones, mechanics arrived to dismantle the auto-buffet vending machines and bookstall staff sorted through the stock to be transferred to Blackpool North.

The ever-present *Evening Gazette* reported: 'A ghost-town atmosphere began to descend on the booking hall when the familiar maroon and white station signs were taken off doors and platform'.

In the left luggage office Tom Pickup, who had worked on the railway for 42 years, was stirring memories while leafing through business records of the network, dating back to the 1880s. Booking office staff were busy sorting through the thousands of unused tickets which would have to be returned to the BR auditing department.

While the customary bustle at Blackpool Central had given way to a strange silence, Blackpool South was reaping the benefit of its overnight 'promotion'. Blackpool South stationmaster T. M. Owen reported that everything was 'going smoothly'. In the event, its Indian Summer was to prove short-lived.

Chapter Nine

TOWARDS THE MILLENNIUM

BY the early 1980s, the Fylde's rail network had reached its nadir. The coastal link through South Fylde had reverted to its original branch line status and seemed destined for eventual closure. Rumours abounded that the main line from Preston to Blackpool North would lose its InterCity links and become just a shuttle service between the two stations. Two of the four pairs of rails between Kirkham and Preston had been lifted in the 1970s. British Rail morale was at rock bottom. The national network was being funded half-heartedly by a Government which made it clear that it believed the railways were a business rather than a public service. BR had to operate within even tighter financial constraints.

Ironically, though, it was this new financial climate that helped to stimulate the modest renaissance in rail services which the Fylde had witnessed since 1985. Fresh financial disciplines demanded new management structures: local managers were given more freedom to take their own decisions as bureaucratic restrictions were lifted. In the Preston area, they used this new found freedom to restructure Fylde services, opening up new routes and travel opportunities. The number of passengers using Blackpool North and Blackpool South doubled between 1985 and 1990 as the two lines were vigorously marketed. Newer, faster and more frequent trains had been introduced on the twin routes. SuperSprinters, for instance, scythed an astonishing 100 minutes off journey times between Blackpool and eastern England. Blackpool North had four InterCity trains daily to London, including the prestigious

Lancashire Pullman, and five in the return direction. As well as intensive services to Manchester and Stockport, destinations included Leeds and York - the Roses link - South Yorkshire and the East Midlands, Liverpool and Buxton. On the South Fylde branch, an hourly service operated to Colne. Sprinters and SuperSprinters operated most of the North services while South relied mainly on the problem-prone Pacers, which had undergone major mechanical improvements after being dogged by technical faults.

However, the 1980s saw road transport extend its grip on the resort even further. In a development which symbolised rail's subservience to road, the route of the former New Line - once the express channel to the town centre - was turned into a link road from the M55 to South Shore, known as Yeadon Way. It now feeds thousands of cars a day during the season into the huge vehicle park laid out on the former Central Station marshalling yards.

The Fylde's least known railway lies beyond the wire fences of British Nuclear Fuels' Springfields plant at Salwick. So when the company heard that railway guard Ray Ruffell wanted to ride on every stretch of railway track in the country - including industrial lines - management invited him to sample a Hudswell diesel shunter. Mr. Ruffell is seen on the foot plate in 1983.

A class 142 Pacer breaks the banner in traditional style to mark the opening of the new Pleasure Beach Station in 1987. The timber-built station was funded jointly by the Pleasure Beach company, BR, Lancashire County Council and Blackpool Borough Council.

If rail is to fight back against the all-pervasive influence of the road lobby on the Fylde coast, it is clear that it will need some so-phisticated weaponry. The most important item in its armoury, rail lobbyists agree, would be electrification. For 30 years, Blackpool politicians and holi-day trade leaders have been cam-paigning for electrification of the line between Blackpool North and Manchester. Wiring-up the line would have cut out the time-consuming change of locomotives at Preston, reducing journey times and improving tourism opportunities. In 1985, the campaign suffered a severe setback when BR announced it was shelving electrification and instead introducing the 75 mph Sprinter units. Today, however, electrification is back on the agenda. BR has confirmed it is carrying out a study into 'infill'

electrification schemes, and Blackpool–Manchester is a top priority. In the summer of 1991, BR chairman Sir Bob Reid con-firmed the scheme was included in the board's 10-year strategy, though its future depended on the government sanctioning the investment. The cost would be about £40 million plus rolling stock – considerably less, in real terms, than the cost of the origi-nal scheme because of cheaper catenary techniques and resig-nalling and track changes al-ready completed. An electrified Blackpool–Manchester line would also provide an important strategic alternative route from Preston when the west-coast main line is blocked and would speed up services to the resort on the proposed Manchester Air-port link, due to open in 1993. The airport line will, in any event, have an hourly service to and from Blackpool North.

As BR experts concluded their 'internal investment appraisal', the future of Fylde electrification was inextricably linked to that of the west-coast main line, the principal InterCity route between London, the North West and Scotland. The line is one of BR's main money-makers, generating a third of InterCity's income and with services covering 13.8 million miles a year. In the summer of 1990, amid a blaze of publicity and simultaneous press conferences in London and the regions, the board announced an audacious £750 million improvement programme for the route by the end of the century. It would include 155 mph locomotives - the InterCity 250s - due to enter service in the middle of the decade, new track alignments and resignalling, making the line compatible with those at the

other end of the Channel Tunnel. While not strictly a part of the scheme, it would be anachronistic if Blackpool-Manchester trains had to continue the laborious process of swapping their sleek class 90 electrics for workhorse class 47 diesels at Preston.

Four months later, though, in October 1990, press speculation began to grow that the west-coast scheme would be shelved or even cancelled. BR had neither the cash of its own, nor sufficient borrowing powers, to include the scheme in its five-year corporate plan, according to the reports. This was deeply embarrassing to the then Transport Secretary, Cecil Parkinson, and Sir Bob Reid, both of whom were under mounting pressure to 'do something' about congested train services. In the Commons, however, Public Transport Minister Roger Freeman emphatically

The futuristic facade of the new Blackpool North Station contrasts sharply with the architectural conservatism of its two predecessors. The awnings were added to the building, opened in 1974, as part of a general refurbishment designed to make it more welcoming to visitors.

denied the scheme had been shunted into a Whitehall siding. The newspaper reports were misleading, he assured MPs.

But further twists in this tortuous rail tale were to come. In May 1991, the new Transport Secretary, Malcolm Rifkind, formally announced an end to 12 years' government antipathy towards the railways, with an 'enthusiastic and unequivocal' declaration that he wished to see a substantial transfer of freight and passengers from road to rail. In the 1991 autumn statement, Mr Major's successor as Chancellor, Norman Lamont, announced a record £1 billion investment to help BR salvage services and improvement

projects that had been cut or postponed by the recession. Even so, it meant BR was still having to sprint simply to stand still.

The controversy has highlighted the deeply flawed nature of BR's funding system. In no other EC country does the Government impose such severe borrowing restrictions on its national rail network, through the prohibitive External Finance Limit. The Treasury demands a guaranteed 8% rate of return on any BR investments, even though their social value cannot be quantified. Otherwise, it has to find investment from its own internal sources - and that usually means higher fares, service re-

Below:
Drivers looked twice as the piggy-back express steamed into the Fylde. Ex-GWR Hall class 4-6-0 No. 4979 'Wootton Hall' was being taken from Barry scrap yard to a new home at the Fleetwood Locomotive Centre, where steam buffs devotedly restored the vintage engine.

Fleetwood's Locomotive Centre, 1990.

ductions or asset sales.

Ominous signs of what lay in store came when BR announced its May 1992 timetable. Instead of four trains from Blackpool to Euston and five in the opposite direction, there were to be just two and three respectively. Inter-City had effectively halved the resort's direct London links. The question was whether the withdrawal of the two lightly-loaded afternoon trains would secure the future of the 6.27 a.m. Lancashire Pullman and the popular 8.35 a.m. The answer came on August 3 in the unlikely location of the passenger lounge on Preston station. The waiting room had been temporarily cleared of passengers while Ivor Warburton, route director of InterCity west coast, announced what had become increasingly likely: after its annual review of services, InterCity was pulling completely

out of Blackpool. All weekday and weekend services were to be withdrawn from 28 September. The news at the press conference was hardly unexpected: rumours had been seeping out of Inter-City's HQ for several weeks.

Mr Warburton spelled out the bleak background to the decision. InterCity profits for 1991-2 had slumped from £49.7 million to £2 million in the wake of the recession, against an overall BR loss of £144.7 million. Privatisation was on the horizon. After a detailed review, InterCity had decided it could not afford to run a peripheral line like Blackpool-Preston. Passenger volumes were low and the cost of switching from electric to diesel for the 18-mile stretch was high. An average of just thirty-one passengers a day were travelling from Blackpool to south of Preston. The Pullman was to be transferred to Lancaster, said Mr Warburton, and Blackpool passengers would be able to connect with an hourly service between Preston and the capital.

On electrification, he denied the InterCity axe would jeopardise the scheme. The decision on electrification would now be based purely on frequent Regional Railways services and not on just two InterCity trains a day. He also hinted the InterCity service could be revived if the line was eventually electrified. He pledged that talks would take place on job prospects for some 30 carriage cleaners with the prospect of relocation at Preston, where cleaning would now take place.

BR coupled the announcement with the disclosure that tenders for the new generation of Inter-City 250 trains for the west coast line had been allowed to lapse. Mr Warburton said it would be wrong 'to keep industry dangling' over the £350 million contract because prospects were not entirely clear. The scheme was dependent on InterCity making enough profit to justify the government making the money available. It also emerged that the seven summer Saturday specials from Edinburgh and Glasgow to Blackpool were to be withdrawn. And there were reports that the two bypass tracks through Kirkham were to be lifted, effectively removing any

Fylde Railways, 1992.

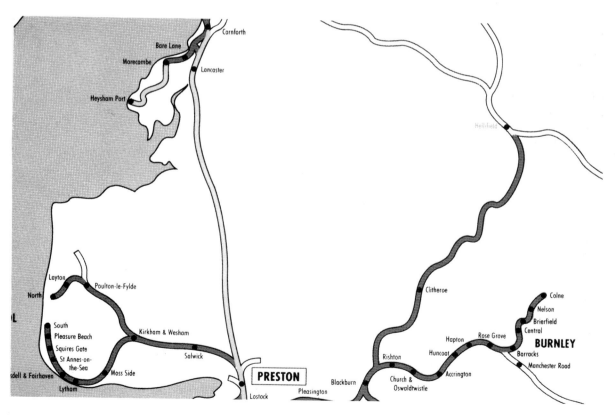

passing point between Blackpool and Preston in the event of locomotive failure.

Immediately, the local newspaper, the *Evening Gazette*, launched a campaign to reverse the axe under the slogan 'InterCity Saver!' Thousands of protests were returned to the paper within the first few weeks of the campaign. An influential cross-party alliance to oppose the cuts was formed by the newspaper, trade unions, councillors, business leaders, tourism operators, rail user groups and MPs. Their case was based on several grounds:

1. The cut would devastate the tourist industry. Although less than 10% of visitors came by rail, this still amounted to a substantial number, many of whom could be put off by having to change at Preston. Disablement groups in particular, were alarmed at the prospect of disabled and elderly passengers having to negotiate the steep steps between the InterCity platforms and the Blackpool services. More than 3 million visitors originate in the South-East and West Midlands - the main markets served by InterCity services to Blackpool. If the passenger count had taken place at the height of the Illuminations, the results would have been dramatically different.

2. The conference trade would be badly damaged. Up to 50% of conference delegates are estimated to arrive by rail. At a time when Blackpool faced growing competition from inland rivals like Birmingham and Glasgow - both on electrified InterCity lines - Blackpool could not afford to pack delegates into two-car Sprinter units for the final leg of the journey.

3. With the Fylde now becoming a centre of technological excellence, the scrapping of the InterCity service would underline the perception of the coast being 'cut off' from the main communications infrastructure.

4. It would further weaken the Fylde's links with the Channel Tunnel, threatening to cut any links between the coast and the continent before they had even begun - in the year of the completion of the single European market.

Richard Branson's Virgin group obviously believed the line had commercial potential: it expressed an interest in running a London–Manchester–Blackpool service from 1994, but user groups were sceptical.

However, InterCity's decision has placed a question mark over the future of the Enfield Road carriage sidings at North Station, where big tracts of land have already been sold.

Though the immediate anger was directed at InterCity, many protesters claimed the ultimate responsibility lay with the government. Its stipulation that InterCity must pay its own way meant that all its lines had to be judged by purely commercial criteria. As Mr Warburton pointed out, InterCity was the only profitable passenger rail network in Europe. The slump in profits and the effect of the recession on passenger numbers meant it had to keep all its services - particularly the so-called peripheral ones - under close review. When services to Shrewsbury and South Humberside were cut, the end of the line appeared inevitable for Blackpool.

The cuts took place against the background of the government's long awaited and much delayed White Paper on privatisation. The final version was much less radical than had been expected before the general election. Then, there had been talk of a Big Bang sell-off, with the entire network being privatised wholesale. Another alternative was the piecemeal privatisation of BR's business sectors. Prime Minister John Major was said to favour a return to a version of the old pre-1948 regional railway companies. In the event, the White Paper published in July was a spatchcock of different measures. The government had decided 'not to move to outright sale of Inter-City services at this stage'. The freight and parcels businesses would be sold to the private sector. For the first time, the operating and track ownership functions would be separated, with a new track authority - Railtrack - set up. Significantly for the Fylde, Railtrack would normally take the lead in promoting new infrastructure investment - including electrification projects. A franchising authority would franchise services to private operators - like Virgin or Stagecoach - on the government's behalf.

There was some relief, however, for those who feared subsidised services - particularly on the South Fylde line - could be badly damaged by privatisation. Transport Secretary John MacGregor pledged that the subsidy to loss-making but socially necessary regional and commuter services would continue under the new system. The White Paper said £629 million of Regional Railways' 1991–92 turnover of £905 million came from grants. Other provisions included the establishment of an independent regulator to protect consumers' interests and also to provide opportunities for the sale or leasing of stations.

However, there was some hope that rail could be allowed a level playing field with road in the future. The government has taken a small step towards including non-monetary benefits, like reducing road congestion and accidents and improving the environment, in deciding on urban rail schemes. Unlike the 8% return which rail projects are expected to provide, roads are assessed on a cost-benefit basis, taking into account non-financial factors. Now, the Department of Transport has said it will take other gains into account rather than just financial returns.

One other big development ripe for exploitation by the Fylde is the Channel Tunnel, due to open in 1993. The prospect of continental trippers travelling direct to Europe's biggest holiday resort has galvanised the Blackpool tourism industry. So far, though, BR's response has been disappointing. It proposes only two trains daily from Manchester, to Brussels and Paris, plus one sleeper from Glasgow via Preston. Electrification of Blackpool North to Manchester Piccadilly would allow the through Chunnel trains from Manchester to 'start back' from Blackpool. Ironically, although the tunnel is on schedule for a 1993 opening, the rolling stock for the North West services is likely to be at least a year late.

Local and cross-country services have fared better than the proposed transnational connections. Their expansion has re-emphasised the umbilical bond between Blackpool's tourism industry and the railway – though, as in the last century, the relationship has not been without friction. In May 1989 BR launched Network NorthWest, its new 'brand image' for lines in Lancashire and South Cumbria. This was accompanied by a major marketing and promotional initiative. At the same time, BR joined forces with Lancashire County Council, one of the more enlightened local authorities in transport terms, to launch the £2.4 million Lancashire Lines project. This involved upgrading 56 stations in the county, including improving access for the disabled, raising platform heights, installing new information boards, providing shelters and removing unsightly graffiti. At Blackpool North, the formerly gloomy concourse has been transformed by new flooring, barriers, frontage and a travel centre. On the South Fylde line,

stations have been spring-cleaned and the Blackpool South terminus, a shadow of its former, self-confident self, has been landscaped and improved. But BR's cash constraints have led to delays in parts of the improvement programme, bitterly disappointing the county council. The Lancashire Lines project is not due for completion until 1994 – three years later than planned.

In fact, the South Fylde branch has probably seen more physical improvement than its big brother. Much of the significant turnabout in the route's fortunes has been due to the efforts of the South Fylde Line Users' Association, which has consistently pressed BR for improvements. As early as 1983, when the line seemed to be withering towards oblivion, a single platform was reopened at Moss Side. Most of the £8,650 bill was picked up by the county. A limited Sunday service was restored and, in 1987, the Blackpool Pleasure Beach Station was opened, providing a direct rail gateway for the millions who visit the amusement park every year. In addition, a 'long line' public address system was being installed to provide service information for passengers on unmanned stations. Lancashire County Council is now actively working for the reopening of Wrea Green station, as part of a county-wide programme of rail development.

In its *Rail Strategy for the North West*, the Railway Development Society calls for consideration to be given to electrifying the route between Blackpool South and east Lancashire. On the main line, the RDS wants the services on the Manchester Airport link to be co-ordinated closely with those to Blackpool. The society also backs SoFLUA pleas for restoration of a single track line to the Blackpool Central site, and suggests that a revived Poulton-Fleetwood service could be combined with upgrading the tram route from Blackpool.

Other proposals for developing the Fylde's rail network are even more innovative. The expansion of light rapid transit schemes, as an environmentally friendly way of moving large numbers of passengers at low cost, has prompted proposals for an advance LRT system on the Fylde coast. A consultant's report by a Liverpool Polytechnic academic, with Lancashire County Council backing, envisaged rerouting and extending the Fleetwood–Blackpool tramway, linking up with the BR line to Kirkham at the Pleasure Beach Station. This would allow interchange of rolling stock between the two systems and relieve congestion on the main roads into South Shore. Interchange is also the theme of a suggested bus-rail terminal on railway land near North Station in Talbot Road, floated by Fylde Friends of the Earth. On an even more ambitious scale, the RDS has proposed a train-plane interchange at Squire's Gate to take advantage of expanding services from Blackpool Airport. The county council has also financed an investigation by the Institute of Transport Studies into the poten-

tial for new stations. Sites investigated included Wrea Green, Saltcotes, Fairhaven, Garstang and Catterall.

The latest, and possibly most innovative, proposal is for a vast light rapid transit 'metro' system covering most of Lancashire, modelled partly on the Manchester Metrolink, which was officially opened by the Queen in July 1992. Brainchild of Lancashire Liberal Democrats, it envisages using mainly existing rail routes to provide a fast, clean and efficient solution to the county's transport problem. It would have the added bonus, say the promoters, of providing hi-tech employment for skilled workers facing redundancy at British Aerospace plants in the county. In the Fylde, the link from Poulton to Fleetwood would be restored, and a number of intermediate stations opened. There would be a direct link to the tram system during the Illuminations and peak tourist seasons. The scheme was relaunched in January 1992 as an alternative to road projects like the £126 million Preston southerly and westerly bypass and the M65 extension.

Despite the bullish attitude of some rail campaigners, BR remains under siege. Regional Railways (formerly the Provincial sector) was established to provide a more devolved, dynamic and responsive management structure. Though the government had made some concessions over the public service obligation grant, used to subsidise loss-making services, the PSO would continue to fall – but more slowly than first planned. Because Regional Railways was operating to such tight margins, little rolling stock could be left idle. Most Sprinter services operated in two- or three-coach sets, which became hopelessly overcrowded at peak periods, so there was little spare capacity for emergencies. Quality improvement teams were introduced to tap staff suggestions for giving passengers – or customers, as they were now known – a better deal. Roger Hammond, passenger services manager for Blackpool and the Fylde, believed he and his staff of almost 300 should concentrate on quality of service despite the problems. He was hoping to build on the achievements of his predecessor Barry Cole, an energetic, marathon-running manager who for five years presided over the coast's railway revival. Prime mover behind many of the improvements was Frank Jones, Regional Railways' bowler-hatted retail manager at Preston.

Regional Railways responded to concern about stock shortages and overcrowding by increasing the length of some peak commuter trains and providing extra services for day trippers. But the middle of 1991 also saw a continuation of the reversal in the relative fortunes of Blackpool and Fleetwood which had first become evident 145 years earlier. A report by the policy research group, the Centre for Local Economic Strategies, opted for Heysham rather than Fleetwood as a west-coast hub for a proposed rail 'landbridge' between the continent, Humberside, the North-West and Ireland. The report said 90% of Fleetwood's income was now from roll-on, roll-off traffic and there was little spare land for port-related development. The CLES said a sober assessment would be that the necessary investment in restoring rail links would be unrealistically high in relation to the likely traffic. However, it said the remaining track between Poulton and Burn Naze could be developed as a tourist line.

Seven miles south of Fleetwood, by contrast, the new Blackpool BR timings offered the prospect of some relief for travellers who had complained of 'cattletruck' conditions. A loco-hauled, large capacity train was provided between Blackpool North and Manchester Victoria in the morning and evening peak periods, an echo of the pre-war club trains, and extra services ran between Blackpool and Victoria during the season. The half-hourly service between Blackpool, Manchester, Piccadilly and Stockport continued, as did the roughly hourly trains on the south Fylde line to Blackburn, Burnley and Colne, with an early morning through train from St Annes to Hazel Grove via Piccadilly.

At peak periods, Blackpool North still remains as much of a railway rainbow as it did in the heyday of the network, with trains in the red livery of the West Yorkshire Metro-Train, the brown of Greater Manchester and the blue and white of Regional Railways. As Blackpool continues to expand, with ventures like the Sandcastle 'inside seaside' and First Leisure's shark-infested Sea Life Centre and Tower World redevelopment, the resort–railway relationship must remain as paramount and pivotal over the next 150 years as it has over the first 150. The loss of the London link makes that far less likely.

Chapter Ten

RAIL-BORN BLACKPOOL

BLACKPOOL was born of the railway. The resort's rail revolution was a unique by-product of the Industrial Revolution, and as such was a sociological, not just a transport, phenomenon. Other towns were the creation of the railway age but, like Crewe or Horwich, developed for geographical or industrial reasons. Other resorts were built by the railway but, like Southport or Morecambe, were the results of middle-class tourism. Blackpool barely existed before the nineteenth century and, after a brief flirtation with middle-class visitors, became the first resort in the world to be founded on mass working-class tourism. It was also Britain's first substantial beneficiary of the democratisation of travel, which allowed working-class passengers to journey on the same trains - albeit in different compartments - as the managerial classes for whom the Fylde became a sought-after dormitory district. It might even be said that Blackpool and the railways,

by providing the poorly-paid, badly-housed proletariat of industrial Lancashire and Yorkshire with a safety valve, helped stave off some of the political unrest that afflicted many of Britain's continental counterparts in the nineteenth century.

The rise of Blackpool from the early part of the Victorian era was largely due to the interdependent but often brittle relationship between the railway, the local authority and private enterprise. Each relied on the other in a mutually fruitful symbiosis, though the railway - because the Fylde was only a small cog in a colossal wheel - was usually the most reluctant partner. Where the railways were most important was in the creation of the classlessness of travel. As Dr Arnold, famous headmaster of Rugby School, watched a Birmingham-London train thunder by, he was elated 'to see it and think that feudality has gone for ever'. Even the disciplinarian Duke of Wellington supported the social liberation provided by the railways. For the first time in history, the poor could travel in the same vehicles, at the same speed, as the rich, though the railway companies ensured that they travelled less comfortably. Railways could not, of course, create leisure time. But they could enable ordinary people to maximise what little leisure time they had. They provided an escape route at a time when towns and cities were filling up at an unprecedented rate.

The Fylde Coast fell within easy reach of the mining towns of the Lancashire-Yorkshire coalfield. It provided a 'lung' through which workers, debilitated by coal or cotton dust, could breathe afresh. The railway also stimulated the development of the Fylde's own industrial belt as cotton mills sprang up alongside the tracks in Kirkham and Wesham.

When the nineteenth century ended, King Cotton had about 400,000 subjects in the Lancashire valleys. Entire towns emptied during the annual Wakes Weeks. Half-miles queues at some stations, where the railway police were frequently called in to control them. A driver, recalled the mad dash when he brought his train into the platform, once counted 24 people in a single compartment. When the crowds reached Blackpool, it was hardly a case of 'getting away from it all' – the view consisted of an ocean of familiar faces. Blackpool was easily the most popular destination, with Southport and Morecambe trailing in its substantial wake. In 1919 about 10,000 victors from Nelson alone stayed in Blackpool for at least four days. Some families were so poor that they bought their own food every day and handed it to their landlady to cook because they could not afford full board.

With the railways – particularly the L & Y – at the apex of their powers, the holiday traffic became a pivotal part of their profitability. It was no coincidence that many of the L & Y's main routes ran east-west, the way the holidaymakers wanted to go. Towns in east Lancashire and west Yorkshire acquired their own routes to the coast, avoiding the congestion of Manchester. Passengers from east of the Pennines could reach the Fylde Coast by way of the link between Todmorden and Burnley and Blackburn, or could follow the route via Rochdale to Bury and Bolton.

Mass working-class travel, and its accompanying social liberations, were phenomena which Karl Marx had failed to account for in his bleak analysis of the development and ultimate collapse of capitalism. The capitalists managed to thwart the 'inevitability' of the forces of historical materialism. Capital was too clever. It would be ludicrous, of course, to claim that a week by the sea for the working classes helped prevent an English Revolution. To employers, however, seaside holidays for their workforces were an example of enlightened self-interest, guaranteeing a healthier, more contented – and therefore more efficient and less restless – body of employees. For many workers, it was the first time they had ventured beyond the boundaries of their own home town. Middle-class reformers also approved because it kept the toiling classes away from the temptations of drunkenness and the traditional urban holiday fairs.

The key to this explosion of working-class travel was the excursion train. Tickets could be as low as a quarter of the price of a scheduled journey, though travelling conditions often matched the rock-bottom fares. The weight of numbers of excursionists was to influence the social character of the resorts they visited, and Blackpool was perhaps the most dramatic example of this. As early as 1851, the *Preston Pilot* newspaper warned:

'Unless immediate steps are taken, Blackpool as a resort for respectable visitors will be ruined . . . Unless the cheap trains are discontinued or some effective regulation made for the management of the thousands who visit the place, Blackpool property will depreciate past recovery.'

These early awaydays came under fire, too, from sabbatarians, who believed they were sacrilegious, though more liberal churchgoers saw it was their Christian duty to help the huddled masses escape from slums and sweatshops on a Sunday. But the opponents were backing a loser. In 1889, 5,000 miners from Barnsley and elsewhere in the south Yorkshire district converged on Blackpool – all, like John Gilpin, 'on pleasure bent'. Barnsley Feast was officially dropped in 1971, but excursions still ran to Blackpool, Cleethorpes, Skegness and Scarborough. Brummies, too, were Blackpool-bound. At Birmingham's New Street Station on August Bank Holiday 1925, thousands of passengers thronged the concourse from the early hours, taking staff by surprise as they tried to board packed excursion trains.

More than a century after Richard Cobden took his entire workforce to Blackpool's newly opened station in 1846, epic works outings to the seaside were still common. In May 1949, Raleigh Industries of Nottingham organised what it claimed to be the biggest works outing since the end of the war. Five thousand cycle-makers – from the managing director to the lowliest apprentice – left for Blackpool at 5am. All employees received 15 shillings with the compliments of the directors. Food rationing was still in force, but each worker received an 'appetising box lunch'. In all, they consumed a mile of sausages in 10,000 rolls, 20,000 sandwiches and 10,000 cakes. The *Nottingham Evening News* showed remarkable enterprise by flying 5,000 copies of that day's paper to Blackpool Airport so the excursionists could read about themselves on the way home. Unlike the modern family, hermetically sealed in its car-cocoon, the trippers enjoyed community singing and games rather than motorway queues and exhaust fumes.

Blackpool has long been Britain's political and trade union

conference capital, hosting the Tory and Labour Party gatherings in alternate years and the Trades Union Congress regularly. Here, too, rail played a central role. The resort rapidly became a popular venue for union gatherings, when politics could be combined with family fun. In 1919, for instance, the Lancashire and Cheshire Miners' Federation held its annual Joy Day and Demonstration at the town's football ground. From 4am to 10am, special services poured into Talbot Road Station every few minutes until a total of 135 trains had safely delivered 100,000 miners and their families. Speakers included the secretary of the Labour Party, Arthur Henderson, and the general secretary of the Miners' Federation of Great Britain, Frank Hodges. The Tower Building opened at 5am, the visitors spent £50,000 in the town – and there was not a single case of drunkenness dealt with by magistrates.

Political party conferences presented the railways with similar logistical challenges, with thousands of delegates, observers, officials and media personnel arriving in the resort. In the years before the Grand Hotel bomb in Brighton in 1984 transformed the policing of party conferences, even the most senior Cabinet figures took a surprisingly relaxed view of their travel arrangements. Prime Minister Harold Macmillan took a scheduled train to one Conservative conference in Blackpool, and gave up his first class seat to two young women laden with children. It is hard to imagine even the egalitarian Mr Major sharing a crowded Sprinter unit with hordes of holidaymakers, not that his security officers would allow him. Today, special trains still run from London for the party conferences, but security officers mingle with the passengers to make sure there are no undesirable on board.

The mass excursion traffic effectively ended Blackpool's claims to gentility. As the working-class colonised Blackpool, the embattled bourgeoisie abandoned it. This suited Blackpool's new proletarian clientele. The resort was undistinguished architecturally or in terms of its natural attributes, apart from its long, straight beach. What they relished was its unpretentious ordinariness. It was Rawtenstall or Rochdale by the Sea, a place, in Stanley Holloway's famous phrase, of 'fresh air and fun'. As late as 1880, Blackpool still harboured lingering hopes of becoming a select watering place. But they were vain hopes. The resort has irreversibly become the ordinary man's holiday destination. Arnold Bennett's Edwin Clayhanger described it as a pleasure city of the poor. During the Wakes Weeks, vast sums were withdrawn from the holiday clubs of the northern mill towns. Traders in Blackpool were delighted by the town's drift downmarket because working-class visitors spent their money more freely than their more sober and discreet social superiors. Today the irony is that, with the decline in manufacturing in the North,

Blackpool's tourism tacticians are trying now to nudge the resort back up-market to fill the gap.

In all this, the railways played the determining role. As they expanded, so did Blackpool – boasting among its assets the Winter Gardens, the piers, Pleasure Beach, Tower, Golden Mile and mor theatres than anywhere beyond Shaftesbury Avenue. And, as Blackpool developed, so did the demands on its railways, which responded reciprocally with expanded services – though the response was sometimes slower than civic leaders had hoped. By the turn of the century, Blackpool had established itself as a resort without compare in meeting the needs of the working man and his family.

But it also developed as a dormitory town, alongside its Fylde Coast neighbours. Less than 90 minutes by train from Manchester, it was ideal for businessmen seeking the best of both worlds – a working life in the country's merchandising capital and a home life by the sea. St Annes, in particular, was an example of this type of development. Before the railway arrived, it simply did not exist. A planned residential town, it developed through the enterprise of a local estate company. In 1881, the population was only 1,000, but it grew ten-fold over the next 30 years. Its spacious detached and semi-detached houses, built from the distinctive, smooth-surfaced Accrington brick, became the residences of those commuting Manchester merchants. Today, many have

been converted into flats or homes for the elderly.

The other main impact of the railway in Blackpool was on the town's geography. Because the railway approached the resort from opposite directions, as a result of the rather haphazard and piecemeal plans of the original pioneers, the town lacked a single focal point – an omission which is still evident today. There is still no real 'town centre' or readily identifiable square to act as the hub of the resort. Instead, the construction of the town's twin termini on the fringes of the central area has resulted in a straggling, unplanned appearance, which contrasts sharply with the symmetry of Fleetwood. A plan to build a direct line between Central and North Stations came to nothing, as described in Chapter Five. Even the disappearance of Central Station has failed to solve this anomaly. Further difficulties for the town were caused by the decision to lay the coast line so close to the sea. It may have been scenic, but the line effectively acted as a boundary between the residential areas to the east and the holiday 'strip' to the west. Despite Blackpool Council's efforts, the geographical barrier bequeathed by the railway remains.

Rail also determined patterns of housing and commercial development in Blackpool. When Talbot Road Station opened in 1846, a glut of guest houses sprang up nearby. But developments of the coastline, including the 1876 decision to switch the Manchester express from Talbot Road to Central, tilted the town's centre of gravity southwards. Property values around Talbot Road slumped and management at Raikes Hall Gardens was forced to put up a large advertisement at Central Station. At the same time, boarding houses began to flourish in the streets around the new station.

Attractions in North Shore were badly hit: some, like the sa-lubrious Claremont Park suburb, fatally. South Shore once more became the select part of town. More than a century later, this north-south divide is still a point of fierce contention among townsfolk.

The railway's legacy has often been beneficial, sometimes detrimental but almost always controversial.

Chapter Eleven

RAILWAY RELICS

ARCHAEOLOGY is as much about railway relics as Roman remains. The branch of industrial archaeology dealing with railways provides a fascinating insight into the economic and social structures underpinning Britain's development as the workhorse of the world. And Blackpool was the paddock where the workhorse was fed, watered and exercised. The Fylde coast is criss-crossed by a poignant pattern of pointers to where the railway once ran. Rusting rails stand as mute memorials to one of the country's busiest railway webs.

The best way to explore the railway archaeology of the Fylde is, naturally, by train - from Blackpool North Station via Kirkham to Blackpool South. The journey has a bleak beginning: the site of the original Blackpool North Station in Talbot Road is now occupied by a supermarket and car park. The passenger of the 1990s faces a longer trek up Talbot Road to reach the new building,

based on the 1938 LMS excursion platforms. The hangar-like entrance hall is a piece of mid-1970s modernism, though BR has made it more welcoming by laying colourful floor tiles and hanging picturesque banners from the ceiling.

Pulling out of the station, our train passes the former coal depot to the left - now the site of a housing development - and yet another piece of sold-off railway land to the right, occupied by a second supermarket. The intricate network of the Enfield Road carriage sidings fans out expansively on the left. Once, the sidings were full of rows of coaching stock; now, so intensive is the use of stock, there is rarely more than a handful of sets to be seen. Whether further stock reductions will remove the *raison d'être* of the depot altogether remains an unanswered question.

After little-altered Layton Station, where the platform levels have been raised to improve accessibility, the train approaches the site of the former Preston-Fleetwood line at Poulton. To the left is the grass-covered track-bed of the old Blackpool-Fleetwood curve. A little further along lies the cutting carrying the abbreviated remnants, protected by catch points, of the Poulton-Fleetwood line, serving ICI Hillhouse. (In Thornton itself, the forlorn remains of the town's former station still stand near a level crossing.) In 1991 the freight line to ICI was renewed with concrete sleepers, and occasional enthusiasts' specials have been organised to Burn Naze, though a new diversionary road is being built on the trackbed at Fleetwood.

After this scene of depressing decline, Poulton Station comes as a scenic surprise. Only a short length of the original platform is in use, but with its eye-catching floral baskets hanging above the passengers, it has consistently finished high in the annual best-kept station competition. Beyond the station, meanwhile, the original 1840 line to Fleetwood once trailed away to the left. Next we pass the site of the former Singleton Station, no trace of which survives. The signal box at Weeton is little more than a hulk; by contrast, the bridge carrying the M55 over the railway is pristine - symbolic, perhaps, of road's dominance over rail.

Nowhere is the shift in transport priorities more apparent than at Kirkham, once the Fylde coast's equivalent of Clapham junction. As our train approaches the station, the deep cutting that used to carry the New Line from Bradkirk to Blackpool can be seen on the

A trio of tank engines at the Lytham Motive Power Museum in 1967. The museum was a little-known but locomotive-rich example of the preservationist's craft. Unfortunately, its exhibits had to be sold in 1992 when recession hit its parent company, Helical Springs, which was on the adjacent site. Some of the exhibits were sold at auction and the rest privately.

right. These days, it is used as a spent ballast tip. All that remains of the flying junction is a short abutment on the left. Instead, the modern-day flyover is a new road bridge of concrete construction carrying the Kirkham and Wesham bypass.

In its shadow at Kirkham North junction, the huge signal box, once the most important on the coast, stands sentinel over the line, with the coastal branch trailing away to the right. On the station approach, the curved neo-classical façade of the Railway Hotel has stood in isolation since the platforms were moved east in 1890. Kirkham and Wesham Station is drastically different from its heyday as the entry-point to the Fylde, several of its yellow and red brick buildings having been demolished. In a £100,000 improvement scheme, the booking office and information services have been moved to

Ansdell and Fairhaven Station has been transformed into little more than an island platform since this picture was taken, but it came into its own during the 1988 Open Golf championship when thousands of spectators used a special shuttle service from Preston to the Royal Lytham and St Annes course.

street level and a new waiting lounge installed – recognition that Kirkham is Lancashire's ninth busiest station. The track-work has been streamlined. To the east is the lightly-used halt of Salwick, which formerly boasted a unique wishing well and has sidings to British Nuclear Fuels' Springfields complex.

Kirkham is the connection point for the South Fylde line.

The compact new station building at St Annes is a model of good, if modest, design, and there are plans to replace the eyesore of the dilapidated landward platforms with a new office block, creating about 90 jobs.

Layton Station – formerly Bispham – is a typical intermediate station, its sturdy architecture contrasting with the minimalism of much modern design. As part of the Lancashire Lines programme involving BR and Lancashire County Council, the platform level has been raised to make it more accessible for disabled people.

Here we swap platforms and board the class 142 Pacer unit for the journey to Blackpool South. Heading out of the station, the passenger can see all that is left of Kirkham's once-extensive goods yard and sidings. Using the old 'up' line, the train enters the single-track branch to Blackpool South. The 'down' line has been lifted and not even a passing loop remains to allow more intensive working of the branch, though the South Fylde Line Users' Association is campaigning for one to be installed. SoFLUA had been formed at a public meeting in April 1982 after BR's decision to withdraw the remaining through services from Blackpool South to Manchester Victoria. The line was left with a shuttle service between Blackpool South and Kirkham – just one train a day went as far as Preston. May 1985 saw the reintroduction of a

through train from Victoria, and the following year all trains were extended to Preston, with several going on to Ormskirk. In August 1987 the Pleasure Beach Station was opened, to the delight of the association. With more than 100 members, it has continued to campaign ceaselessly for further improvements, under the leadership of chairman Paul Nettleton, secretary Vernon Smith and vice-chairman Malcolm Richardson. Installation of the passing loop remains top of SoFLUA's shopping list: the association believes this could be done in 1994–5, when the Fylde's ageing semaphore signalling system is due to be replaced.

As our train heads south-west, the first landmark is the picture-postcard village of Wrea Green, whose attractive station closed in 1961. Today, it is as if the station never existed, though SoFLUA is pressing for its reinstatement to serve what is becoming a fast expanding community. Only a mile away is the first intermediate station on the line – Moss Side – reopened as a replacement for the original halt which was closed at the same time as Wrea Green. Like most stations on the line, it is unmanned.

Next stop is Lytham, once the nerve-centre of the coastal line. During the 1970s it declined into a virtual ruin, but the imposing façade has now been sympathetically refurbished as part of an up-market pub-restaurant development. According to the BR Property Board, disused station buildings are successfully being converted into wine bars, restaurants and pubs all over the North-West, with the property sales generating valuable income for cash-strapped BR. Experience at Lytham, however, has shown that these rail-into-restaurant schemes are not always guaranteed money-makers: the Porters pub, built in the shell of the station, was put on the market four years after being opened in the £600,000 joint enterprise between Fylde Council and the private sector. After a further £80,000 refurbishment, it is now

The run-down buildings of Lytham Station in 1984, with the track yet to be singled. During the 1970s the once-imposing station declined into a virtual ruin.

After:
Today, the building has been sensitively refurbished as part of a pub-restaurant scheme. Note that one of the tracks has now been lifted.

known as the Station Tavern, serving 'Guard's Mushroom' and the 'Stationmaster's Lunch'.

The car park to the left of Lytham Station was once a bay platform from which the railmotor service to Blackpool Central departed. Perhaps the saddest symbol of the decline of the railway in south Fylde – and of the remorseless impact of the recession – was provided by the auction in March 1992 of a unique collection of railwayana at the Lytham Motive Power Museum. The Dock Road museum, which featured five historic locos, had been opened to the public in 1969 by Jim Morris, managing director of the adjacent company, Helical Springs. Mr. Morris was forced into the sale reluctantly by the need to keep the recession-hit parent company on the rails. Though the auction raised £66,000, only one of the locos was sold under the hammer: the rest were entered in a postal auction. A 105-year-old former North British Railway tank engine went to the Scottish Railway Preservation Society for a bargain £15,000. The dispersal of the collection provides a poignant postscript to the eclipse of the railway and the rise of the recession.

Heading west, our Pacer unit – perhaps a descendant of the railmotor – approaches Ansdell and Fairhaven Station, an island platform which boasted substantial buildings until destaffing in March 1971 and demolition a year later. Now, with the help of the County Council, the platform has been resurfaced and new seats and a waiting shelter provided. The station's potential was amply demonstrated by the Open Championship at Royal Lytham and St Annes in 1988, when thousands of spectators used a special shuttle service from Preston to Ansdell.

The reopening of Moss Side Station in 1983 amounted to a vote of confidence in the South Fylde line, which had seemed destined for ultimate closure. The unmanned station was a replacement for the original halt on the line which was closed in 1961. Most of the cost was met by Lancashire County Council.

With its distinctive canopies and long platform – reputed to be one of the longest outside the big cities – Poulton Station retains some of the pride and ebullience of the railway's heyday. This 1980 picture shows the Blackpool-bound track passing under the road bridge, before curving sharply to the left towards Blackpool North and right to Burn Naze. With its hanging baskets and pristine appearance, Poulton-le-Fylde – to give the station its full title – has won many best-kept BR building awards.

Next stop is St Annes, where the well-designed new station on the left contrasts starkly with the vandalised and dilapidated remnants of the landward platform buildings, closed in 1983. Ambitious £600,000 proposals for a buffet bar and restaurants were granted planning permission but a drinks licence was refused. Fylde councillors were told that an appeal was in the pipeline, but the developers subsequently withdrew it. Meanwhile, the platform remained one of the area's saddest eyesores, and by the summer of 1991 the building was under threat of demolition. Early in 1992, however, it was revealed that a Cheshire-based property company was negotiating with BR to buy the station buildings for a £1.5 million office development that would create about 90 jobs. Despite some opposition, Fylde Council approved the plan.

Approaching the Blackpool boundary, the train calls at Squire's Gate, wedged between the airport and the sprawling Pontin's holiday centre. For many years, the station was home for Blackpool's 'camping coaches' – caravan-style converted carriages – but the sidings which housed them are long gone. The journey from Squire's Gate to Blackpool South and Central was one of the most exhilarating on British Railways, as holiday expresses thundered along, parallel with the sea, towards the Pleasure Beach and Golden Mile. It remains a unique run, even in its foreshortened form. But the width of the track-bed, now occupied by just a single line, gives a clue to how busy the route once was. Tell-tale smoke stains on bridge parapets provide a still-discernible reminder of the age of steam. As the train rattles through South Shore, it reaches the new Pleasure Beach

Kirkham and Wesham is, in fact, a misnomer. The station, for topographical reasons, was sited in Wesham, so it should theoretically be called Wesham and Kirkham. The station has undergone a major improvement programme, with some surplus buildings being demolished, and the booking area given a cheerful face-lift. The £100,000 scheme has seen information services being moved up to street level and the installation of a comfortable new waiting lounge.

Station, site of the original Burlington Road halt, and passes beneath the rebuilt footpath leading to the guest houses to the east of the line. Then it is on towards Blackpool South.

Passing beneath the final road-bridge, with its soot-smeared parapet, the traveller can, with difficulty, locate the outline of the original South Shore station site. Today, the only easily visible landmarks are a cobbled approach road and a weed-encrusted strip where the station once stood.

Station Road, Station Terrace and the elegant Grand Hotel (now holiday flats) bear witness to the way it used to be. To the right, the Yeadon Way link road sweeps into view to connect with a giant coach and car park. It must have been awe-inspiring to approach Blackpool along the New Line, across an otherwise pancake-flat landscape. Today, it pours its travellers onto a sea of asphalt. The single rail line is squeezed onto the car park's western extremity, and even the arch beneath the Waterloo Road bridge has been filled in, as if to protect tarmac's territory from any railway encroachment. A rusting buffer-stop marks the end of the line, and a single platform is all that is left of the original, extensive station. The road-level buildings have been demolished. Under the Lancashire Lines scheme, however, the station has been spring-cleaned and a new passenger shelter installed. Beyond Blackpool South is a swathe of land that used to house the 34 parallel sidings serving Blackpool Central. Now it is one of Europe's biggest vehicle parks. The sturdy iron bridges that carried the railway over intervening roads now reverberate to the vibrations of millions of cars and coaches.

But it is the Central Station site itself that provides the most poignantly nostalgic views. Unrecognisable as the location of one of Britain's most intensively used railheads, it is tantalisingly close to the attractions of the Golden Mile. Railway wraiths still stalk the site. The outline of the filled-in platforms is clearly visible beneath the wheels of the ranks of parked cars. Tragicomically, as highlighted in Chapter Seven, the only station building still standing is the toilet block – the coppers from which were reported to have paid the station's rates bill! Lavatories are apparently the one need that rail travellers and car users have in common. The nearby railwaymen's hostel, once earmarked as a YMC complex, has been transformed into holiday flats. And, of course, an amusement complex occupies part of the site. But Queen Victoria, and her subjects who pioneered rail travel in Blackpool, would undeniably not have been amused.

BIBLIOGRAPHY

Ashcroft, B., *Beside the Seaside, 1959* (published in *Steam World,* July 1990).

Awdry, C., *Encyclopaedia of British Railway Companies* (Patrick Stephens Ltd., 1990).

Baker, M. H. C., *Railways to the Coast* (PSL, 1990.

Curtis, B., *Fleetwood – A Town is Born* (Terence Dalton, 1986).

Davies, R. K., *Companion to the Fylde* (Countyvise, 1982).

Eyre, K., *Fylde Folk: Moss or Sand* (Dalesman, 1979).

Faith, N., *The World the Railways Made* (The Bodley Head, 1990).

Foster, D., *Excursions into Fylde History* (Hendon Publishing).

Holt, G. O., *A Regional History of the Railways of Great Britain,* vol. 10, the North West (David and Charles, 1978).

Hooper, R. (ed.), *The Fylde Story* (Fylde Borough Council, 1988).

Jordan, A. and E., *Away for the Day* (Silver Link, 1991).

Jowett, A., *Jowett's Railway Atlas of Great Britain and Ireland* (Patrick Stephens Ltd., 1989).

Kirkman, R. and Van Zeller, P., *Rails to the Lancashire Coast* (Dalesman, 1991).

Marshall, J., *Forgotten Railways: North West England* (David and Charles, 1981).

Marshall, J., *The Lancashire and Yorkshire Railway,* vols 1, 2 and 3 (David and Charles, 1969, 1970, 1972).

Mitchell, W. R., *Lancashire Milltown Memories* (Dalesman, 1987).

Nock, O. S., *The Lancashire and Yorkshire Railway: A Concise History* (Ian Allen, 1969).

Palmer, S. and Turner, B., *Blackpool by Tram* (Palmer and Turner, 1968).

Parkin, G. W., *60,000 Trippers a Day* (published in the *Railway Magazine,* October 1967).

Parry, K., *The Resorts of the Lancashire Coast* (David and Charles, 1983).

Railway Development Society, *A Rail Strategy for the North West* (Railway Development Society, 1989).

Railway Development Society, *A–Z of Rail Re-openings* (Railway Development Society, 1989).

Ramsbottom, M., *The Preston and Wyre Railway* (Hedgehog Historical Publications, 1991).

Rothwell, C., *The Fylde in the 1930s and '40s* (Hendon Publishing, 1984).

Rothwell, C., *Over-Wyre in Times Past* (Chamberlain Publishing, 1990).

Rothwell, C., *The Preston and Wyre Railway* (Winckley Publishing, 1991).

The files of the *Evening Gazette,*
Blackpool, and *Blackpool
Gazette* and *Herald.*

Tramway Museum Society, *The
Blackpool Tramway* (Tramway
Museum Society, Crich,
Derbyshire, 1981).

Turner, B., and Palmer, S., *The
Blackpool Story* (Palmer and
Turner, 1976).

Wells, J., *Railways and Holidays*
(published by Backtrack,
July–August 1991).

Wood, A. W. and Lightbown, T.,
*Blackpool in Old Picture
Postcards* (European Library,
1983).

Young, T. (ed.), *Lancashire and
Cumbria by Rail* (Railway
Development Society, 1987).